D0343718

# ILLUSTRATED
## ENGLISH SOCIAL HISTORY

I  Fox Hunting

# ILLUSTRATED
# ENGLISH SOCIAL HISTORY

## VOLUME FOUR

### *The Nineteenth Century*

by

## G. M. TREVELYAN, O.M.

*Master of Trinity College, 1940-51*
*Formerly Regius Professor of Modern*
*History in the University of Cambridge*

---

## *ILLUSTRATIONS SELECTED BY*
## *RUTH C. WRIGHT*

---

## READERS UNION
## LONGMANS, GREEN AND CO
### LONDON 1958

LONGMANS, GREEN AND CO LTD
6 & 7 CLIFFORD STREET LONDON W I
THIBAULT HOUSE THIBAULT SQUARE CAPE TOWN
605–611 LONSDALE STREET MELBOURNE C I

LONGMANS, GREEN AND CO INC
55 FIFTH AVENUE NEW YORK 3

LONGMANS, GREEN AND CO
20 CRANFIELD ROAD TORONTO 16

ORIENT LONGMANS PRIVATE LTD
CALCUTTA BOMBAY MADRAS
DELHI HYDERABAD DACCA

BIBLIOGRAPHICAL NOTE
*First published in U.S.A. and Canada* 1942
*First published in Great Britain* 1944
*This volume first published* 1952
*Second Impression* 1957

*Photogravure plates printed by*
JARROLD & SONS LTD. NORWICH

*Colour plates printed by*
EDMUND EVANS LTD.

*Text printed in Great Britain by*
SPOTTISWOODE, BALLANTYNE & CO. LTD.
*London & Colchester*

*This* RU *edition was produced in* 1958 *for sale to its members only by Readers Union Ltd at* 38 *William IV Street, Charing Cross, London, W.C.2, and at Letchworth Garden City, Hertfordshire. Full details of membership may be obtained from our London address. The book is set in* 11 *pt Garamond type leaded and has been reprinted by Spottiswoode, Ballantyne & Co. Ltd. The photogravure plates were printed by Jarrold & Sons Ltd, Norwich, and the colour plates by Edmund Evans Ltd. The book was first published in the U.S.A. and Canada in* 1942 *and in Great Britain in* 1944. *The illustrated edition was first published in* 1949 *by Longmans, Green & Co. Ltd.*

To the memory of
### EILEEN POWER
*Economic and Social*
*Historian*

# PREFATORY NOTE TO THE
# ILLUSTRATIONS

THE illustrations selected for this fourth and last volume bring the social picture up to 1901.

The illustrated record of the Eighteenth Century in Volume III has already reflected the development in range and spirit from the previous centuries, but the Nineteenth Century provides a difference even more significant, at least in so far as the latter half of the century is concerned.

The period covered in Volume IV runs from the 1790's to the death of Queen Victoria, and therefore moves from the age of the French Revolution and the Napoleonic Wars, through the gay licence of the Regency to the more soberly coloured middle years of the century, in which industrial unrest contrasts sharply with the rise in industrial wealth and material comfort, and comes finally to the feverish activity and elegance of the *fin de siècle*.

But such a summary obscures the tremendous counterpoint of enterprise and blindness, of opportunities seized or neglected, that lies behind the century, a pattern which can only be spotlighted here and there—imperial development overseas and industrial conditions at home, the railway age and the neo-Gothic fervour, agricultural reform and the internal combustion engine.

The harsh contrasts of the mediaeval world though transmuted are yet recognizable in Victorian England. Sir Gorgius Midas flourishes oblivious of King Cholera's Court (§75 and §119), the 'back-to-backs' mock the success of the Great Exhibition (§69 and §77), the child labourers of the textile factories go unheeded among the cheers that greet the abolition of negro slavery (§93, §94 and §95). It is easy to lay overmuch emphasis on this aspect and thereby to ignore the very great and real achievements of the century, not only in colonization and industrial output but in thought and literature and invention. I have sought therefore to strike a balance between them and while not ignoring the rick burner and the slum dweller to show as well the other side of the picture, the achievements of engineering, the high standard of living that could be enjoyed by a greatly increased number, the lavish scale of entertainment and amusement, and, perhaps the most dominant feature of all, the great figures that hold the century together and are themselves the expression of its virtues and its faults—Dickens and Thackeray, Ruskin and Carlyle, Darwin, Gladstone, William Morris, Tennyson and the rest.

The type of social illustration and the medium change with the scene: the early years of the century glow with hand-coloured aquatints, in the thirties and forties the lithograph, the woodcut, and engraving are used to picture the industrial and the fashionable scene alike. The whole century is rich in satire from Gillray and Rowlandson through Leech and Doyle to du Maurier, with what contrasted effect these examples of their work will disclose.

The narrative painter and engraver dominate the latter half of the century, with the black-and-white artist, the journalist and the photographer commenting increasingly on the social scene of the contemporary world: the trend is either sentimental or plainly factual, until the sense of design and composition reasserts itself in the new medium of photography.

I have to thank Mr. C. K. Adams, Director of the National Portrait Gallery, for his continued help on the portraits chosen, and Miss Hamilton Jones, Librarian of Aerofilms, Ltd., for making available to me the Victorian photographs reproduced at §115 and §131–134, as well as for drawing my attention to the aerial photograph of industrial housing (§69).

RUTH C. WRIGHT
*Illustrations Editor*

# CONTENTS

*Prefatory Note to the Illustrations*

*Introduction*

# ILLUSTRATIONS

# INTRODUCTION

This fourth and last volume of the Illustrated Edition of my English Social History covers the Nineteenth Century. Its principal theme is the economic causes and social and intellectual consequences of the Industrial Revolution in full blast. By the end of Victoria's reign it had given increased material comforts to an enormously enlarged population. It had done so by substituting machine production for craftsmanship, and the modern great city for the village as the normal residence of Englishmen. The consequent changes in the ethos of civilization and intellect form, I confess, too large, intricate and varied a theme for the brief space that can here be afforded. But if this volume is patently inadequate, I hope it may at least be suggestive.

# ACKNOWLEDGMENTS

THE publishers' grateful thanks are due to all those who have given permission for photographs to be taken of the MSS., printed books, pictures or antiquities in their care or ownership, or have allowed photographs in their possession to be reproduced. In particular the publishers wish to acknowledge the permission of the Proprietors of *Punch* to reproduce drawings by George du Maurier and John Leech. Full details of such ownership, etc., will be found in the descriptive notes for each item.

## Chapter One

### COBBETT'S ENGLAND, 1793–1832

1. *Change in Town and Country—Factories—Working-class conditions—*
   *Colonization—Education—Luddites—Trade Unions.*

   (*The Wars with France,* 1793–1815. *Waterloo,* 1815. *Peterloo,*
   1819. *The Reform Bill,* 1831–1832.)

BETWEEN the classical world of the Eighteenth Century
with its self-confidence and self-content, and the restless
England of Peterloo and the rick-burnings, of Byron and Cobbett,
were interposed twenty years of war with Revolutionary and
Napoleonic France (1793–1815).

Coming at a critical moment in our social development, the
long war was a grave misfortune. With its violent disturbances of
economic life, and its mood of 'anti-Jacobin' reaction against all
proposals for reform and all sympathy with the claims and
sufferings of the poor—the war formed the worst possible environment for the industrial and social changes then in rapid
progress. The modern English slum town grew up to meet the
momentary needs of the new type of employer and jerry-builder,
unchecked and unguided by public control of any sort. A rampant
individualism, inspired by no idea beyond quick money returns,
set up the cheap and nasty model of modern industrial life and its
surroundings. Town-planning, sanitation and amenity were
things undreamt of by the vulgarian makers of the new world,
while the aristocratic ruling class enjoyed its own pleasant life
apart, and thought that town building, sanitation and factory
conditions were no concern of government. Great cities would
in any case have been bad enough as the slums of Eighteenth
Century London had already shown, but the circumstances
of the Napoleonic period in England were peculiarly unfavour-
able to the better development of the grim factory towns of
the North, and to the relations of the new type of employer to
the new type of employee. Man had acquired formidable tools

I

for refashioning his life before he had given the least thought to the question of what sort of life it would be well for him to fashion.

Since municipal lethargy and corruption had long lost all touch with civic traditions and public spirit of mediaeval corporate life, the sudden growth of the new factory quarters did not disturb the slumbers of the town oligarchies, who were so well accustomed to neglect their old duties that they were incapable of rising to a new call. And when, as usually happened, the development took place outside the area of any corporate town, the gentlemen magistrates of the County made no pretence to control housing activities.

When Waterloo was fought, rural England was still in its unspoilt beauty, and most English towns were either handsome or picturesque. The factory regions were a small part of the whole, but unluckily they were the model for the future. A new type of urban community was permitted to grow up which it was fatally easy to imitate on an ever increasing scale, until in another hundred years the great majority of Englishmen were dwellers in mean streets. When, as the Nineteenth Century advanced, local government was gradually made to attend to its duties, by being subjected to democratic local election and to central control from Whitehall, then indeed large provision was made for health, convenience and education. But even after these belated reforms in the utilitarian sphere, ugliness remains a quality of the modern city, rendered acceptable by custom to a public that can imagine only what it has seen.

The course of the Napoleonic wars, with blockade and counter-blockade, made business a gamble. There was every incitement to manufacturing enterprise, except security. England's control of the sea, and her new power of machine production, not yet imitated in other lands, gave her a monopoly of many markets in America, Africa and the Far East. But the European markets were alternately opened and closed to British goods according to the vagaries of diplomacy and war. One year an allied State would have its armies clothed and shod by British workmen: next year it might be under the heel of France, a part of Napoleon's 'continental system.' The unnecessary war with the United States (1812–1815) was another element of disturbance to trade.

The sufferings of the English working class were increased by these violent fluctuations of demand and employment; and unemployment was worst of all during the post war slump after Waterloo.

The war had also the effect of shutting out the supply of European corn, which had at last become necessary to steady food prices in our thickly populated island. Wheat rose from 43 shillings a quarter in 1792, the year before the war broke out, to 126 shillings in 1812, the year Napoleon went to Moscow. The poor, both in town and country, suffered terribly from the price of bread, though it put money into the pockets of tenant farmers, freehold yeomen, and receivers of tithe and rent. During the twenty years of war, the extent and character of land cultivation was adapted to these high prices, so that when corn fell at the return of peace many farmers were ruined and rents could not be paid. In these circumstances the protective Corn Law of 1815 was passed, with the aim of restoring agricultural prosperity at the expense of the consumer. It encountered the most violent opposition from the town population of all classes irrespective of party. The landlord members of Parliament complained that, as they went down to the House to vote for the Bill, they had been savagely mauled by a mob set on 'by the inflammatory speeches of Baring the banker, and the false statements of the Lord Mayor of London.' (Sir R. Heron's *Notes*, ed. 1851, p. 50) For a generation to come, until the Repeal of the Corn Laws in 1846, the question of agricultural protection divided England, and gave a political focus to the differentiation between urban and rural life which the Industrial Revolution was making more marked every year, as the inhabitants of the town lost all touch with the farming, and the inhabitants of the village with manufacture.

The observant eyes of Defoe, as he rode through Queen Anne's England, had been pleased by the harmony of the economic and social fabric. It was shattered now, giving place to a chaos of rival interests, town against country, rich against poor. A hundred years after Defoe, another horseman, William Cobbett, on his 'rural rides' noted the new symptoms; the wrongs of the disinherited poor inspired his headlong, single-handed crusade against the phalanx of their oppressors. The poor, perhaps, had in reality always been as poor and as ill used; but their evil plight became more obvious to themselves and to others, now that they were segregated and massed together. In the past, poverty had been an individual misfortune; now it was a group grievance. It was a challenge to the humanitarian spirit which the Eighteenth Century had engendered. That spirit had been obscured for a while by England's angry fright at the French Revolution, but in the new Century it could no longer regard the victims of economic circumstance with the hard indifferent eye of earlier ages. So Cobbett's blustering words had weight. [See § 1.]

The poor suffered by the war. [See § 3.] But at no period had the landed gentry been wealthier or happier, or more engrossed in the life of their pleasant country houses. The war was in the newspapers, but it scarcely entered the lives of the enjoying classes. [See § 4, 5.] No young lady of Miss Austen's acquaintance, waiting eagerly for the appearance of Scott's or Byron's next volume of verse, seems ever to have asked what Mr. Thorpe or Mr. Tom Bertram were going to do to serve their country in time of danger. For in those happy days the navy was a perfect shield to the safety and to the amenities of island life. While Napoleon was ramping over Europe, the extravagance and eccentricity of our dandies reached their highest point in the days of Beau Brummell, and English poetry and landscape-painting enjoyed their great age. [See § 6, 7, 8.] Wordsworth, whose mind had, in time of peace, been aroused and disturbed by the French Revolution, so completely recovered his equanimity during the long war that he was able to produce a body of philosophic poetry expressive of

> central peace subsisting at the heart
> Of endless agitation,

a mood which it is more difficult to catch and keep under the conditions of modern totalitarian warfare.

During half the years of the struggle with France, England sent no expeditionary force to Europe, and even the seven campaigns of the Peninsular War cost less than 40,000 British dead: the blood tax was a light one for all classes. Mr. Pitt's income tax was more vexatious, but rent and tithe had risen with the price of corn, so that landowners did well upon the balance. The 'gentlemen of England' beat Napoleon, the professional, and they deservedly won praise and prestige for a victory which, not being abused, gave us the priceless boon of a hundred years' immunity from another 'great war.' But the gentlemen had fought and conquered the upstart on very easy terms for themselves, and so in the years that followed the restoration of peace they were, somewhat ungratefully perhaps, denounced by the rising generation of reformers as having been war profiteers.

> See these inglorious Cincinnati swarm,
> Farmers of war, dictators of the farm;
> *Their* ploughshare was the sword in hireling hands,
> *Their* fields manured by gore of other lands;
> Safe in their barns, these Sabine tillers sent
> Their brethren out to battle. Why? for rent!
> Year after year they voted cent for cent,
> Blood, sweat, and tear-wrung millions—why? for rent!
> They roar'd, they dined, they drank, they swore they meant
> To die for England,—why then live? for rent!
>                                (Byron, *The Age of Bronze*, 1823.)

If the war proved a source of increased wealth to the landlords and of prolonged calamity to the wage-earner, it was a gamble to 'the middling orders of society': it made this merchant a profiteer, like old Osborne in *Vanity Fair*, and that other, like poor Mr. Sedley, a bankrupt. As a whole, 'the nation of shopkeepers' longed for peace, to bring security, to open the European markets once for all and to reduce taxation. But they had no thought of surrender to Bonaparte. [See § 2.] Many of the wealthier—the bankers, the old-established merchants and moneyed men, and their families—shared the Tory politics of the 'quality,' to whose society they were admitted, with whom they married, and from whom they bought seats in Parliament and commissions in the army. But many a manufacturer of the new type, himself or his father sprung from the yeomen or from the working class, more often than not a Dissenter, his thoughts engrossed by the factory he had built beside some Pennine stream, had no love for the aristocracy, and dumbly resented the war as something from the glory and interest of which he was excluded. Such men were making the new wealth of England, but they had no part in her government either central or local, and they were jealous of the haughty class that kept them out. They felt too little sympathy with the real victims of the war, their own employees—as little indeed as the landlords and farmers felt with the ill-fed workers of the field whose labour filled their pockets so full. It was a hard world of sharply divided interests, with small sense of national brotherhood, save occasionally in face of the foreign foe.

For all that, we must not exaggerate the actual amount of discontent, particularly in the first part of the war. The democratic movement, inspired by the original French Revolution and the writings of Tom Paine, was suppressed in the ' 'nineties,' quite as much by public opinion as by government action: working-class mobs in Birmingham and in Manchester sacked the chapels and houses of the Dissenting reformers, and the Durham miners burnt Tom Paine in effigy. In the bulk of the working class, discontent only grew slowly as a result of very real suffering, and for a long time it was sectional and regional, not national. Even during the period of anti-Jacobin repression, when it was 'safer to be a felon than a reformer,' the majority of Englishmen were still proud of themselves as being a free people. In the year of Trafalgar, a distinguished American scientist, visiting the London theatres, notes that

Enthusiastic applauses were bestowed by the Galleries this evening on this sentiment, that if a poor man had an honest heart there lived not one in England who had either the presumption or the power to oppress him. In this incident may be seen the active jealousy of liberty which exists even in the lowest orders of England.[1]

It is to be feared that the 'sentiment' was unduly optimistic, but the fact that it could be applauded by the 'gallery' is not without pleasant significance.

Bread and cheese became, in many southern counties, the staple diet of the labourer, washed down with beer or tea. They seldom saw meat, though many grew potatoes in the cottage garden. The danger of sheer starvation with which the rural poor were faced in many districts owing to war prices and low wages, was averted by a remedy that brought much evil in its train. In May 1795 the magistrates of Berkshire were summoned to meet at Speenhamland, a northern suburb of Newbury, for the expressed purpose of fixing and enforcing a minimum wage for the county in relation to the price of bread. It would have been a difficult policy to carry out against the resistance of recalcitrant farmers,

[1] B. Silliman's *Travels in England in 1805*, New York 1810, I, p. 252.

during a period of violent price fluctuations; but in principle it was the true remedy. If it had been adopted for Berkshire and for all England, it might have diverted our modern social history into happier channels. It was the right course, and it was appointed by ancient custom and existing law. Unfortunately, the J.P.s who had come to Speenhamland for this good purpose, were there persuaded not to enforce the raising of wages but to supplement wages out of the parish rates. They drew up and published a scale by which every 'poor and industrious person' should receive from the parish a certain sum per week in addition to his wages, so much for himself and so much for other members of his family, when the loaf cost a shilling. As the loaf rose, the dole was to rise with it. This convenient scale, vulgarly known as the 'Speenhamland Act,' was adopted by the magistrates in one county after another, till the evil system was established in perhaps half rural England, particularly in the Counties of recent enclosures. The Northern Counties were among those outside the system, for in the North the near neighbourhood of factories and mines tended to keep up rural wages by competition.

This payment of rates in aid of wages relieved the large employing farmer from the necessity of giving a living wage to his workpeople, and most unjustly forced the small independent parishioner to help the big man, while at the same time it compelled the labourer to become a pauper even when he was in full work! The moral effect was devastating on all concerned. The large farmers were confirmed in their selfish refusal to raise wages, the independent classes staggered under the burden of the poor-rate, while idleness and crime increased among the pauperized labourers. An American observer wrote with too much truth in 1830:

The term pauper as used in England and more particularly in agricultural districts, embraces that numerous class of society who depend for subsistence solely upon the labour of their hands.[1]

It is not, however, true, as was thought at the time, that rates in aid of wages were an important cause of the rapid rise of

[1] Between 1792 and 1831 poor-law expenditure in the County of Dorset increased 214 per cent., expenses for prosecutions for crime 2135 per cent., whilst the population had only increased 40 per cent. (*Victoria County History, Dorset*, II, 259). In 1813 more than seven millions were raised in all England for poor-rate, while local taxation for all other purposes only amounted to one and a half millions.

population which Malthus was teaching his contemporaries to dread so much. In the Nineteenth as in the Eighteenth Century, the rise of population was due not to an increase in births but to a decrease in deaths. Not the foolish magistrates of Speenhamland but the good doctors of Great Britain were responsible for the fact that between 1801–1831, the inhabitants of England, Wales and Scotland rose from eleven to sixteen and a half millions.

The price of corn during the war, while it starved and pauperized the labourer, not only benefited the landlord and large tenant farmer, but for a time checked the decline of the freehold yeoman and the copyhold peasant. [See § 13.] But after Waterloo, with the crash in corn prices, the reduction in the ranks of the small cultivators was resumed. It was upon them that the Speenhamland system weighed hardest financially, for in many Southern Counties, particularly in Wiltshire, the numerous farmers who employed no paid labour themselves were forced to pay heavy poor-rates in order to eke out the wages paid by the large employing farmers, their rivals who were destined to supersede them. And the small cultivator still suffered by the continued enclosure of the open fields and commons, and by the progressive decline of cottage industries.

Yet we must not exaggerate the pace and extent of change. The Census of 1831 shows that out of just under a million families engaged in agriculture, nearly 145,000 were those of owners or farmers who hired no labour, as against 686,000 families of field labourers for hire. That is to say, on the eve of the Reform Bill, the agricultural proletariate proper were only two and a half times as numerous as the independent cultivators of the soil. And there was still a 'small peasantry' left, almost as numerous in fact as the farmers who paid wages to employees. But much the greater part of the acreage cultivated was now in the hands of the large farmers, and the open fields and commons had for the most part gone.

Once the war and its reactions were well over, it appears from statistical calculation of real wages that the agricultural labourer was no worse off in 1824 than he had been thirty years before, taking the average of the country as a whole.[1] In some regions he was decidedly better off. But his standard of life had declined in

---

[1] See Clapham, *Ec. Hist of Modern England*, I, pp. 125–131.

those parts of the rural South which lay farthest from the wage-competition of factories and mines, particularly where the poor-rates were being employed to keep wages down, and where the labourer depended on the farmer who employed him for the clay-built hovel in which he lived. He was often forced to take part of his wages in bad corn and worse beer. In those counties rick-burning and rioting gave expression to the sense of hopeless misery. In earlier and simpler days the labourer had more often been lodged in the farm and ate at the board of the farmer. This had meant of course, that he was just as dependent on his employer as when in later times he was provided with a tied cottage. But it had meant also a closer and often therefore a kinder personal contact, and less segregation of classes. Cobbett speaks of the old-fashioned labourer sharing his employer's meal on equal terms, except that the farmer might reserve for himself a stronger brew of beer.

In the winter of 1830, a few months before the introduction of the Great Reform Bill, the starving field labourers of the Counties south of Thames marched about in a riotous manner demanding a wage of half a crown a day. The revenge taken by the Judges was terrible: three of the rioters were unjustly hanged and four hundred and twenty were torn from their families and transported to Australia, as convicts. Such panic cruelty showed how wide a gap of social misunderstanding divided the upper class from the poor, even when the anti-Jacobin spirit had been exorcised from the political sphere and ' Reform ' had become the watchword of the King's ministers. (Hammond, *Village Labourer*, chaps. XI and XII.)

It would, however, be a great mistake to regard the unhappy condition of the labourers in the Counties south of Thames as characteristic of all rural England. In the North, and indeed in all regions where factory life and mines were expanding, the wages even of agricultural labourers were higher, the poor-rate lower, and the number of people in receipt of poor relief less. The average standard of life was almost certainly higher than in the previous century, if all regions and all classes are taken into account. Not only Cobbett but everyone else, complained that farmers were 'aping their betters,' abandoning old homely ways, eating off Wedgwood instead of pewter, educating their girls and dashing about in gigs or riding to hounds. Whether this was good or bad depends on the point of view, but in any case it was a 'rise in the standard of life.'[1]

And among humbler rural classes there was much happiness and some prosperity, varying with place, year and circumstance. [See § 14.] The life of the village children, let loose to play in the hedges, heaths and thickets, was wholesome and sweet, as Bewick, Wordsworth and Cobbett recorded from their own boyhoods' experience in the previous generation, and Howitt in the new century. William Howitt, George Borrow and other writers who shared the life of the common people in lane, field and cottage in the 'twenties and 'thirties, leave an impression of much widely diffused health and happiness as well as much hardship.[2] Village sports and traditions, and the daily contact with nature— and nightly contact too in the surreptitious taking of hares and rabbits in their hedgerow runs by 'old Hobden's' ancestors—how are these things to be assessed in computing the 'condition of the rural poor'? And how is the great variety of life in different counties and regions, on different estates and farms to be reduced to the compass of a single generalization?

As far back as 1771 Arthur Young had deplored the fact that, with better facilities of travel, the drift of country lads and lasses to London was on the increase. But now other towns were also

---

[1] The change in the farmer's life was complained of in the Waterloo period, and thirty years later the complaint was still being made as these verses, written in 1843, show:

*Old Style.*
Man, to the plough;
Wife, to the cow;
Girl, to the yarn;
Boy, to the barn,
And your rent will be netted.

*New Style*
Man, Tally Ho;
Miss, piano;
Wife, silk and satin;
Boy, Greek and Latin,
And you'll all be Gazetted.

Lord Ernle (*English Farming*, p. 347) is scornful of these charges, not as wholly untrue, but as inadequate to account for agricultural distress; he observes that this explanation of farmers' difficulties is 'as old as the hills,' and that in 1573 Tusser had alluded to farmers who neglected their business in order to go hawking.

[2] Howitt's delightful *Rural Life in England* and *Boy's Country Book* cover experiences from 1802 to 1838; Borrow's *Lavengro* records experiences from 1810 to 1825.

drawing away their thousands from all parts of rural England. The movement was most marked in the North, the region of mines and factories and cotton mills. Indeed, the Census figures for 1801 to 1831 show that some outlying parishes in the North were already diminishing in population every decade. This was not yet true of the average English village; but although a rural parish in the first thirty years of the Century might show no drop in the number of its resident inhabitants, it was none the less sending many of its young people to the Colonies or United States, or to the centres of industry and commerce at home.

The continual rise in the population made it indeed impossible to provide work for everyone in the English village. Agriculture had absorbed all the hands it required. And many traditional kinds of rural occupation were disappearing. Great national industries, like cloth, were migrating back out of the country districts to which they had moved in the later Middle Ages and Tudor times. The village was becoming more purely agricultural; it was ceasing to manufacture goods for the general market, and, moreover, was manufacturing fewer goods for itself.

With the improvement of roads and communications, first the lady of the manor, then the farmer's wife and lastly the cottager learnt to buy in the town many articles that used to be made in the village or on the estate. And a 'village shop' was now often set up, stocked with goods from the cities or from oversea. The self-sufficing, self-clothing village became more and more a thing of the past. One by one the craftsmen disappeared—the harness maker, the maker of agricultural implements, the tailor, the miller, the furniture maker, the weaver, sometimes even the carpenter and builder—till, at the end of Victoria's reign, the village blacksmith was in some places the only craftsman left, eking out a declining business in horseshoes by mending the punctured bicycle tyres of tourists! The reduction in the number of small industries and handicrafts made rural life duller and less self-sufficient in its mentality and native interests, a backwater of the national life instead of its main stream. The vitality of the village slowly declined, as the city in a hundred ways sucked away its blood and brains. This century-long process had already begun between Waterloo and the Reform Bill.

But the English village during the first half of the Nineteenth Century was still able to provide an excellent type of colonist to new lands beyond the ocean. The men were accustomed to privation and to long hours of out-of-door work, and were ready to turn their hands to tree-felling, agriculture and rough handicraft. The women were ready to bear and rear large families.

All the circumstances of post-war England helped the great movement of colonization. The over-population that terrified the contemporaries of Malthus, the economic and social troubles, the resentment felt by the freer spirits against the rule of squire and farmer, were all factors that went to build up the Second British Empire, filling Canada, Australia and New Zealand with men and women of British speech and tradition. 'In Canada,' wrote one immigrant, 'we can have our liberty, and need not be afraid of speaking of our rights.' 'We have no gamekeepers and more privileges,' wrote another. The Scots, too, Highlander and Lowlander alike, had discovered the Canadian trail. The forests fell, the log huts rose and the rich wilderness began its yield of crops and men. In Australia in the early decades of the Nineteenth Century, capitalist 'squatters' introduced cattle and sheep farming on a large scale, and opened out an attractive field of enterprise for adventurous spirits. The settlement of New Zealand came a little later, chiefly between 1837 and 1850, being somewhat more regularly organized by the zeal of Gibbon Wakefield and by the pious efforts of Anglican and of Scottish Presbyterian committees. The Briton of the Hanoverian and early Victorian era was a villager, or was only at one remove from the villager: he was not wholly a product of the city, incapable of going back to the land, or of plying more trades than one. He was still able to adapt himself to the hardships of pioneer life, and to its variety of requirements and opportunities. And so the British Commonwealth of Nations was founded just in time.

But while many English villagers were crossing the ocean, many others were drifting into the industrial districts at home. During the Napoleonic Wars this movement within the island had been specially marked. The age of 'coal and iron' had come in earnest. A new order of life was beginning, and the circumstances under which it began led to a new kind of unrest. [See § 15, 16, 17.]

Immigrants to the mining and industrial districts were leaving an old rural world essentially conservative in its social structure and moral atmosphere, and were dumped down in neglected heaps that soon fermented as neglected heaps will do, becoming highly combustible matter. Very often their food, clothing and wages were less bad than they had been in the farms and country cottages they had left. And they had more independence than the agricultural labourer whose wages were eked out by poor relief. But migration to the factories had meant loss as well as gain. The beauty of field and wood and hedge, the immemorial customs of rural life—the village green and its games, the harvest-home, the tithe feast, the May Day rites, the field sports—had supplied a humane background and an age-long tradition to temper poverty. [See § 14.] They were not reproduced in mine or factory, or in the rows of mass produced brick dwellings erected to house the hands. The old rural cottages whence they came had indeed often been worse places to live in materially—picturesque but ruinous and insalubrious. Yet it was not impossible to have some feeling for a rickety window embowered in honeysuckle, or a leaking roof that harboured moss and doves! Wordsworth's 'Poor Susan,' the exile in the great city, remembered the country cottage where she was born,

> The one only dwelling on earth that she loves.

Such affection could not be transferred to town slums. It cannot even to-day be felt for the model workman's flat.

The worst slums in the new urban areas were those inhabited by the immigrant Irish. They came from rural slums far worse than those of the worst English village, and brought with them proportionately bad habits. England's treatment of the Irish peasant was perpetually being avenged over here. But the worst period for sanitary conditions in the industrial regions was the middle of the Nineteenth Century rather than the beginning, because so many of the new houses had then had time to become slums, since no one repaired or drained them as the years went by.

The factory hands, like the miners, were brought together as a mass of employees face to face with an employer, who lived apart from them in a house of his own in a separate social atmosphere; whereas under the old rural system they had been scattered about —one, two or at most half a dozen hands to each farm—in close and therefore often in kindly personal relation with their em- ployer the farmer, at whose board the unmarried hands took their meals, cooked by the farmer's wife.

The mass of unregarded humanity in the factories and mines were as yet without any social services or amusements of a modern kind to compensate for the lost amenities and traditions of country life. They were wholly uncared for by Church or State; no Lady Bountiful visited them with blankets and advice; no one but the Nonconformist minister was their friend; they had no luxury but drink, no one to talk to but one another, hardly any subject but their grievances. Naturally they were tinder to the flame of agitation. They had no interest or hope in life but Evangelical religion or Radical politics. Sometimes the two went together, for many Nonconformist preachers themselves imbibed and imparted Radical doctrines. But the political conservatism with which the Wesleyan movement had started was not yet exhausted, and acted as a restraining element. In the opinion of Elie Halévy, the great French historian who wrote for us the history of the English Nineteenth Century, the power of Evangelical religion was the chief influence that prevented our country from starting along the path of revolutionary violence during this period of economic chaos and social neglect:

'Men of letters disliked the Evangelicals for their narrow Puritanism, men of science for their intellectual feebleness. Nevertheless during the Nineteenth Century, Evangelical religion was the moral cement of English society. It was the influence of the Evangelicals which invested the British aristocracy with an almost Stoic dignity, restrained the plutocrats who had newly risen from the masses from vulgar ostentation and debauchery, and placed over the proletariat a select body of workmen enamoured of virtue and capable of self-restraint. Evangelicalism was thus the conservative force which restored in England the balance momentarily destroyed by the explosion of the revolutionary forces.' (Halévy, *Hist. of English People*, transl. by E. I. Watkin, III, p. 166.)

But there is another reason, besides the restraints and consolations of a powerful popular religion, to account for the moderate character and the limited success of the Radical movement in the generation after Waterloo. It is true that it swept over the factory districts, but the factory districts were still a relatively small part of England. In 1819 factory conditions were not widely spread outside the Lancashire cotton area, and the Radical movement was therefore capable of being temporarily suppressed by the Peterloo massacre and the Six Acts. The future lay with the factory system, but for the present the great majority of the English working class were still employed under the old conditions of life, whether in agriculture, in industry, in domestic service, or in seafaring. Peterloo was an important event, because that unhappy charge of the Yeomanry, sabre in hand, among the cotton operatives of Manchester disgusted the rising generation of Englishmen with anti-Jacobin Toryism. But the victims of Peterloo though they were a class typical of South Lancashire, were not typical of the England of that day.

Mr. Pickwick's world, the world of the fast stage coaches and of the First Reform Bill, was a transition world, combining the old with the new economic society, and the old still predominated. The agricultural labourers and the industrialists in small workshops still for a while outnumbered the miners and factory hands. [See § 9, 10, 12.] And then there were the great army of men and women in household service. In the third decade of the century the female domestic servants alone were 'fifty per cent. more numerous than all the men and women, boys and girls, in the cotton industry put together.' (Clapham, I, p. 73.) The conditions of work and wages for domestic servants have been little examined by economic or social historians, and would indeed be very difficult to assess, for they varied greatly from house to house according to the occupation and character of the employer. [See § 18, 19.] Mr. Samuel Weller, as we all know, was a peculiarly favoured specimen of his class, with 'little to do and plenty to get.' He and his Mary ('Housemaid to Mr. Nupkins') were not Radicals by outlook or tradition, though they probably cheered for the Reform Bill.

Another large class, equally far removed from factory or domestic employment, was the mobile army of unskilled labour known as 'navvies' engaged in gangs that moved from place to place, digging canals,[1] making roads and in the next generation constructing embankments and tunnels for railways. [See § 20, 21.] In the North, the Irish were found in their ranks in great numbers; but in the South they consisted almost entirely of the surplus labour of English villages, which in those parts had fewer outlets to factories and mines. Some highly paid engineers were officers in the army of navvies, and were specially numerous and highly rewarded when it came to railway construction and the

---

[1] Hence the term 'navvies,' for 'inland navigators.'

piercing of tunnels. But as a whole the 'navvies' were among the least skilled, the most ignorant and the least well paid of the new industrial classes. They were the nomads of the new world, and their muscular strength laid its foundations.

At the opposite end of the ranks of labour were the skilled engineers and mechanics. The men who made and mended the machines were the *élite* of the Industrial Revolution and its true body-guard. They were better paid than their fellow-workmen, they were on the average more intelligent, and they took the lead in educational movements. They were respected by their employers, who had to consult them and to bow to their technical knowledge. They were in the forefront of progress and invention, and rejoiced in the sense of leading the new age. Such workmen were the Stephensons of Tyneside; there was nothing 'middle class' about the origins of the man who invented the locomotive, after having taught himself to read at the age of seventeen.

It is indeed easier to reconstruct the early history of the coal-miners and textile hands, than that of the mechanics and engineers, because the latter were scattered up and down the country. But any picture of the earliest and worst stage of the Industrial Revolution is too black if it omits the life of the mechanics. The motto of the coming age was 'self-help,' a doctrine that left behind many of the weaker and less fortunate; but there were from the first other classes beside employers and middlemen who reaped a share of its benefits, and who grew to a larger manhood under the moral and intellectual stimulus of the individualist doctrine.

Adult Education received its first impetus from the Industrial Revolution in the desire of mechanics for general scientific knowledge, and the willingness of the more intelligent part of the middle class to help to supply their demand. It was a movement partly professional and utilitarian, partly intellectual and ideal. Disinterested scientific curiosity was strong among the better class of workmen in the North. From 1823 onwards Mechanics' Institutes, begun in Scotland by Dr. Birkbeck, spread through industrial England. The flame was fanned by the bellows of Henry Brougham's organizing and advertising genius, in the period of his greatest public service, when he stood for the real 'Opposition' in Parliament and country, pointing to the future and its needs. Self-satisfied classical scholars like Peacock might

§1 William Cobbett

§2 Jack Tar settling Buonaparte

JOHN BULL, going to the WARS.

JOHN BULL, Happy.

JOHN BULL'S glorious Return.

JOHN BULL'S Property in danger.

JOHN BULL'S PROGRESS

§3 "The poor suffered by the war". John Bull's Progress

§4 The Temple of the Muses, Finsbury Square

§5 Draper's shop, Pall Mall

"The war was in the newspapers, but it scarcely entered the lives of the enjoying classes"

§6 Sir Walter Scott

§7 William Wordsworth

§8 "Crossing the Brook" by Turner

"*There was a time when meadow, grove and stream,*
*The earth and every common sight,*
*To me did seem*
*Apparelled in celestial light,*
*The glory and the freshness of a dream.*"—WORDSWORTH

§9 The Wensley Dale Knitters (1814)

§10 The Cloth Dressers (1814)

§11 The Factory Children (1814)

§12 The Sheffield Cutler (1814)

§13 The Lord of the Manor receiving his rents

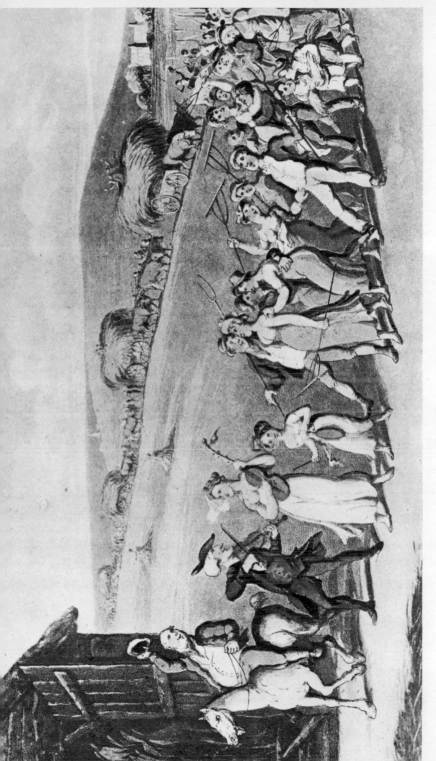

£14 Harvest Home

§15 The Collier (1814)

§16 In a coal mine (1844)

§17  Pit head at Church Pit, Wallsend (1844)

519 The servants' dinner

§20 A canal and lock gates (in 1819) at Stoke Hammond, Bucks.

§21 Entrance to the tunnel of the Liverpool and Manchester Railway at Edge Hill (1831). Navvies at work

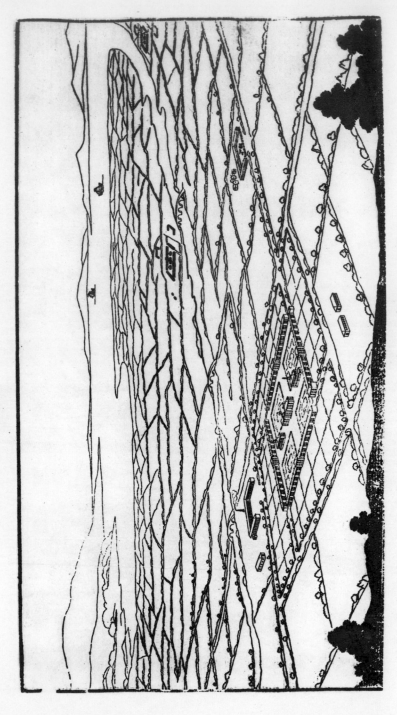

§22 Robert Owen's plan for the agricultural and manufacturing villages of Unity and Mutual Co-Operation (1817)

laugh at the 'learned friend' and his 'steam-intellect society,' but the new world could not live wholly on classical scholarship carefully locked away from common use in the close ecclesiastical corporations of the Oxford and Cambridge of that day. Nor, in an age that needed first and foremost to be converted to see the need for education, was there so much harm in this 'semi-Solomon, half knowing everything,' but irrepressible in zeal as a propagandist and not afraid of making a fool of himself before the learned if he could help the ignorant to learn.

The success of these Mechanics' Institutes, with an annual subscription of a guinea, showed that whatever was happening to other classes of workers, prosperity was coming to the engineers and mechanics from the Industrial Revolution which had called them into being. Francis Place, the Radical tailor, had seen the first efforts of the working classes at self-education crushed in the anti-Jacobin panic a generation before; but in 1824 he described his pleasure at seeing 'from 800 to 900 clean respectable-looking mechanics paying most marked attention to a lecture on chemistry.' That year the *Mechanics' Magazine* sold 16,000 copies; and 1500 workmen subscribed a guinea apiece to the London Institute. Encyclopaedic knowledge was now circulated in cheap books and periodicals by enterprising publishers, and was absorbed by eager students in garret and workshop.

While adult education and self-education were on the move before a strong new breeze, the foundation of London University (1827) was inspired by the same spirit. [See § 64.] Nonconformists and secularists, excluded from Oxford and Cambridge, had drawn together to found an undenominational teaching centre in the Capital, on the basis of keeping theology out of the curriculum, and having no religious tests for teachers or taught. The tendency of the embryo university was towards modern studies, including science. The strict classical curriculum was identified in men's minds with the close educational establishments of the Church and State party. 'Utility' appealed more to the unprivileged city population. The founding of London University was therefore an educational event of the first importance, but at the time its real significance was lost in sectarian and partisan recrimination, and not a little good-humoured satire of Brougham and his 'cockney college.'

Primary education both lost and gained by the religious and

denominational squabbles, characteristic of an age when Dissenters had become numerically formidable, but Churchmen were still unwilling to abate a jot of their privileges. On the one hand public money could not be obtained for educating the people, because the Church claimed that it must be spent under the aegis of the State religion, and the Dissenters would not agree to the use of public funds on such terms. On the other hand, the hostile denominations vied with each other in collecting money voluntarily for the erection of Day Schools and Sunday Schools. Readers of Miss Brontë's *Shirley* will remember the scene (chap. XVII) of the rival school feasts, when the column of Church schoolchildren, 'priestled and women officered,' its band playing *Rule, Britannia!*, marches at quick step down the narrow lane and scatters the column of Dissenting school children and their pastors, who raise a feeble hymn and then turn tail. In that comedy we have the secret of much in old English politics, religion and education.

'The British and Foreign School Society,' under Dissenting and Whig Patronage, worked on the basis of undenominational Bible-teaching, while the Churchmen countered by the foundation of the 'National Society for the Education of the Poor according to the Principles of the Church of England.' The 'National' or Church schools became the most usual mode of popular education in the English village.

Though much was lacking in the organized education of that age as compared to our own, very many people of all classes at the time of Waterloo knew the Bible with a real familiarity which raised their imaginations above the level of that insipid vulgarity of mind which the modern multiplicity of printed matters tends rather to increase than diminish.

With the growth of new industrial conditions, involving the disappearance of apprenticeship and of the personal relation of the journeyman with his employer, Trade Union action was essential to protect the interest of the employee, especially as the State refused any longer to carry out its old Tudor policy of fixing wages. But during the anti-Jacobin period (1792–1822) all combinations of workmen, whether for political or for purely economic purposes, were regarded as 'seditious.' The only wonder is that this attitude on the part of the State as bottle-holder to the employer did not lead to more violence and blood-shed. It did lead to the 'Luddite' trouble.

In the middle of the Napoleonic wars, unemployment, low wages and starvation were periodic among the industrialists of Nottinghamshire, Yorkshire, and Lancashire, partly owing to the first effects of new machinery. In 1811–1812 the 'Luddites' began to break the frames on a systematic plan of action. Although there was a tendency to violence among some Irish in the Luddite ranks, there was no likelihood of a serious rebellion, and the fear of one was simply due to the absence of any effective police in the island. For that reason alone, resort had to be made to the soldiers to repress the mobs and protect the machines. The non-existence of a civilian police aggravated the symptoms of political and social disturbance, and was a direct cause of the Peterloo tragedy. Peel's initiation of the famous blue-coated corps, with its top hats and truncheons, in the year 1829 was the beginning of a better state of things. Formed in the first instance for the London area, 'the new police' saved the Capital, during the Reform Bill agitation two years later, from suffering at the hands of Radical mobs as Bristol and some other towns suffered, and as London itself had suffered from the Gordon riots fifty years before. As Peel's police were gradually established throughout the whole country, riot and the fear of riot ceased to have their former importance in English life.

But there was another aspect of the movement of 1812 besides machine-breaking. The Luddites demanded, by the legal method of petition to Parliament, that existing laws, some as old as the reign of Elizabeth, should be put into force for the State regula-tion of wages and hours fairly as between employer and employed.[1] This was a perfectly just demand, the more so as these ancient statutes were being partially enforced to prevent combinations of workmen to protect their own interests: indeed, the position had recently been strengthened against working-class Unions by Pitt's Combination Act of 1800. The laws were supposed to apply against combinations both of masters and men, but in fact the masters were allowed to combine as freely as they wished, while their employees were prosecuted for strike action. Finally,

---

[1] In fact, since the middle of the Seventeenth Century, the fixing of wages by magistrates, when it was resorted to at all, had been the fixing of a maximum wage only and therefore of no use to employees.

in 1813 Parliament repealed the Elizabethan statutes which gave magistrates power to enforce a minimum wage.

To leave the workman unprotected by the State as to wages, hours and factory conditions, while denying him the right to protect himself by combination was frankly unjust. It was not *laissez-faire*, but liberty for the masters and repression for the men. The high pundits of the *laissez-faire* doctrine, such as Ricardo, were on the side of the employees in this matter, demanding the legalization of Trade Unions.

After 1822 the anti-Jacobin tide at last began to ebb. With Peel at the Home Office, repression ceased to be the sole method of government, and in 1824-1825 the House of Commons, in the spirit of a new and better age, was induced by the skilful lobbying of Joseph Hume and Francis Place to repeal Pitt's Combination Act and make Trade Unions legal. Henceforth the various forms of working-class association and corporate action grew up rapidly as a normal and recognized part of the social structure, instead of becoming revolutionary as they must needs have done if the Combination Act had remained in force.

It must not be supposed that the strife of classes was ever an absolute thing in England, or that all masters were harsh to their workpeople or indifferent to their hardships. An enlightened minority of employers had supported the legalizing of Trade Unions. And during the Napoleonic wars, the enterprising manufacturer, Sir Robert Peel the elder, father of a greater son, had begun to agitate for State control of the conditions of children in factories, especially for the protection of the pauper apprentices, in whom a horrible slave traffic was carried on by the public authorities. [See § 11.] No doubt the good Sir Robert, who himself employed 15,000 hands, was in part anxious to restrain the unfair competition of his more unscrupulous rivals. But the Factory Acts of the period before the Reform Bill were not only very limited in scope, but remained dead letters for want of any machinery to enforce them.

Unfortunately, in the earlier years of the Century, State control in the interest of the working classes was not an idea congenial to the rulers of Britain. They turned a deaf ear to Robert Owen when he pointed out to them that his own New Lanark Mills were a model ready to hand, to teach the world how the new industrial system could be made the instrument of standardized improvement in sanitation, welfare, hours, wages and education, raising the conditions of working-class life to an average level that could never have been attained under the domestic system. Let the State, said Owen, enforce similar arrangements in all factories. But the world, though sufficiently interested to visit and admire the New Lanark Mills refused to imitate them. Men were still unable to comprehend the modern doctrine which Owen first clearly grasped and taught, that environment makes character and that environment is under human control. [See § 22.] The great opportunity that his vision had perceived was missed, until in the slow evolution of a Century the State has come round to his doctrine of the control of Factories and the conditions of life for all employed therein, which he had vainly preached to the Cabinet of Liverpool and Castlereagh. At the end of the Nineteenth Century, partly by successive Factory Acts, partly by Trade Union action, factory life had proved a means of raising standards, while the 'sweated' domestic trades, like dressmaking which could not be brought under factory control, were still for a while longer the scene of the worst oppressions, especially of women.

To form a true picture of the processes of social change going on in the post-war period, we must avoid the mistake of supposing that the working classes as a whole were financially worse off than before the Industrial Revolution, although their grievances being of a new kind were more resented, and their complaints were more vocal than in the past. Professor Clapham, the greatest authority on the economic history of the period, roundly condemns

the legend that everything was getting worse for the working man, down to some unspecified date between the drafting of the People's Charter and the Great Exhibition. The fact, that after the price fall of 1820–1 the purchasing power of wages in general—not, of course, of everyone's wages—was definitely greater than it had been just before the revolutionary and Napoleonic wars fits so ill with the tradition that it is very seldom mentioned, the work of statisticians on wages and prices being constantly ignored by social historians. (Preface to the *Economic History of Modern Britain*.)

This is true and important; but the purchasing power of wages is not the whole of human happiness, and for not a few the amenities and values of life were less than those enjoyed by their rural forefathers.

## Chapter Two

### COBBETT'S ENGLAND, 1793–1832

**2.** *Women and the new world—The fund-holders—Religion—Shipping—Navy and Army—Sporting events—Game Laws—Humanity.*

THE growth of the factory system and of capitalist agriculture involved a number of changes in the employment of women, which altered conditions of family life, and therefore in the long run affected the relation of the sexes.[1]

From the earliest ages of mankind, women and children had conducted certain industries in the home, and the variety and complication of cottage manufactures had increased in Stuart and early Hanoverian England. Their sudden decay, owing to the invention of new machines, was of profound consequence to the life of the poor. The first result, in the closing years of the Eighteenth Century, was much unemployment and misery for single women, and the breaking up of many small rural households whose budget had always been balanced by the earnings of the wife and children.

The move to the factories could not be effected at once, and in many cases was not effected at all. During the Napoleonic Wars women, deprived of their old means of livelihood by the decay of cottage industries, went into field work beside their men folk. [See § 23.] The big capitalist farmers began to employ gangs of women in hoeing and weeding. Such employment had always been occasional among country women, and they had always turned out at haytime and harvest. But the big farmers in the age of Speenhamland employed females all the year round, because the newly enclosed lands required much weeding and preparation; because there was less charge on the poor-rate if the wife earned wages as well as the husband; and because if women were drawing pay it helped to keep down the wages of the men. It was

[1] Many facts relative to this subject will be found in Dr. Ivy Pinchbeck's *Women Workers and the Industrial Revolution*, 1930.

22

a vicious circle: the fact that the husband's wages were not at that time enough to support the whole family forced the wife and daughters into this competition with the men for farm service. It was only as the field labourer's wages gradually rose in the second half of the Nineteenth Century, and as agricultural machinery enabled farmers to dispense with many kinds of hand work, that female employment in agriculture again became as restricted as it had been in earlier times.

Under the old system of life, many village women took an active part in tilling the family patch of ground, looking after the pig or cow, marketing the goods or helping to conduct some small local business: in the England of the past, as in the France of to-day, the wife was often her husband's partner and fellow-worker. But the growth of high farming and big business tended to drive women out of these activities, turning some of them into 'ladies' of no occupation, others into field-labourers or factory hands, others into workmen's wives entirely devoted to the care of the home.

As in most changes in human affairs, there was gain as well as loss. The working-class home often became more comfortable, quiet and sanitary by ceasing to be a miniature factory: for example, the removal of the picking and cleaning of cotton from the cottage to the mill made many huswifes happier and many homes more pleasant.

Moreover, the women who went to work in the factories, though they lost some of the best things in life, gained independence. The money they earned was their own. The factory hand acquired an economic position personal to herself, which in the course of time other women came to envy. This envy, based on the aspiration to independence, was not confined to girls of the working class. It came to be felt also in higher circles. By the middle of the Nineteenth Century, members of the leisured class like the Brontë sisters and Florence Nightingale were beginning to feel that the independent factory hand, earning her own bread, was setting an example that might be of value to the 'lady.'

For the early Victorian 'lady' and her mother of the Regency period, too often had nothing in the world to do but to be paid for and approved by man, and to realize the type of female perfection which the breadwinner of the family expected to find in his wife and daughters.[1] No doubt the ever increasing numbers of leisured women usefully enlarged the reading public and the patronage of art and literature. Indeed, leisured women, like Jane Austen, Maria Edgeworth and Hannah More, had time and education enough to become authors and artists themselves. That was good. But many of the young ladies who doted on Scott's and Byron's romances, and strove to look like their heroines, were suffering from too much leisure. Fashions in art and literature, as they pass, affect the habits of life and sometimes even the appearance of the more sophisticated classes. Scott's pseudo-mediaeval ideals of the 'lady' worshipped by the enamoured hero, and Byron's sultanic vision of woman as odalisque, helped to inspire the artificial uselessness of the would-be fashionable sisterhood. [See §24, 25, 26.]

As the upper and middle classes grew richer, and as the rural gentry fell more under the influence of town life, it became a point of social pride that the young ladies should be taught by a governess in the schoolroom, and thence pass to the drawing-room, and do at all times as little domestic work as possible. The ladies in Miss Austen's novels, representing the smaller gentry and upper bourgeoisie, have little to do but to read poetry, retail local gossip and await the attentions of the gentlemen. To be sure it was different in the great political families: in Lansdowne or Holland House a lady's life was by no means so limited or so dull.

Moreover, 'ladies' were not encouraged to exercise their bodies except in dancing. Very few women at this period hunted; that became more usual in the strenuous Victorian days, as we see in *Punch's* pictures and in Trollope's novels. The lady of this earlier period was expected to keep herself in cotton wool. When Elizabeth Bennet walked three miles in muddy weather and arrived at Netherfield 'with weary ankles, dirty stockings and a face glowing with warmth and exercise,' Mrs. Hurst and Miss Bingley 'held her in contempt for it.' Even in the hardy North, Wordsworth in 1801 wrote a poem, as its title tells us, to console and encourage 'A Young Lady, who had been reproached

[1] Before the Married Women's Property Acts of the late Victorian period, a woman's property became her husband's at marriage. The law was in curious contrast to the words of the marriage service, when the man was made to say 'with all my worldly goods I thee endow.' It was really the other way round.

for taking long walks in the country'! It was all very absurd, for in less artificial classes of society, women were walking long distances to and from their work; there were Welsh women who annually walked the whole way to London and back in pursuit of seasonal employment in the fruit and vegetable gardens round the Capital.

The upper-class woman was being devitalized and cut off from life and its interests, as a result of the increasing wealth of her men folk and the more artificial conditions of modern life. In the old self-supplying manor-house, with its innumerable jobs to be done within and without doors, the ladies of good family, like the Pastons and Verneys, had had their allotted tasks. But now it became the hall-mark of a 'lady' to be idle.

There were, of course, even among the well-to-do, many women who lived active and useful lives, some of the old domestic type; others, like Hannah More's, of a modern, philanthropic and intellectual variety. But there lay a real danger for the new century in the false ideal of the 'sheltered' lady. And in a snobbish society like England, where those below were always seeking to imitate those just above them, the false ideal spread downwards among the smaller bourgeoisie now multiplying in the new suburbs of the towns.

Even in the countryside the wives of wealthy farmers were accused of setting up as 'ladies,' too fine to work. In old days the farmer's wife had always been (as she usually is to-day) a very busy woman, with all the cares of the house and some of the cares of the farm on her shoulders. In dairy farms she was herself the foreman labourer, getting the milkmaids up before sunrise and often working on at butter or cheese making until a late hour at night. Dairy farming, especially in the regions of the West that supplied the London market with cheese and butter, was the most arduous and the most profitable of the occupations of women. On other farms the wife was more occupied with housework. She had to cook and care not only for her own family but for the labourers who fed at her husband's board and lodged under his roof. She was a hard-working woman with little leisure.

But in the early Nineteenth Century these domestic conditions had changed on the large enclosed farms of the new order. The hands employed were more numerous, but for that very reason they no longer boarded or fed with their employer. The farmhouse, as Cobbett complained, was becoming 'too neat for a dirty-shoed carter to be allowed to come into.' The big farmers engaged a better type of domestic servant to relieve their wives of drudgery and to give a gentlemanlike appearance to the parlour, even if the kitchen was still usually preferred for family life on ordinary occasions. The farmer's daughters, it was said, 'instead of being taught their duty and the business of a dairy at home, receive their education at a Boarding School, are taught to dance, to speak French and to play upon the harpsichord.' [See § 27.]

But this was only true to its full extent in the case of the wealthier farmers, some of whom were indeed gradually becoming gentlemen. The farming class included a number of different social grades and standards. The farmers in the North did not ape the gentleman like some farmers of the Speenhamland regions. The northern 'hind' was more independent than the pauperized labourer of the South, and the social demarcation between him and his employer was less marked; this was specially true of the moorland shepherds. And all over England there were still thousands of farms where the women of the family took a share in all kinds of work, and many where the farm hand still fed with those who employed him.

An account of women's life at this period ought to include a reference to the great army of prostitutes. It had existed in all ages, and its ranks had grown with the increase of wealth and population in the country. Except for 'rescue work' which the pious were now actively taking in hand, the evil was left untouched. It infested the towns without the least public control; 'the harlot's cry from street to street' made public resorts hideous at nightfall. The growing 'respectability' of the well-to-do classes in the new era diminished the numbers and position of the more fortunate 'kept mistresses,' who had played a considerable part in Eighteenth Century society. But for that very reason the demand was increased for the common prostitute who could be visited in secret. The harshness of the world's ethical code, which many parents endorsed, too often drove a girl once seduced to prostitution. And the economic condition of single women forced many of them to adopt a trade they abhorred. The decay of cottage manufacture starved orphan girls till they bowed the head for bread. Low wages in unregulated sweated industries made temptation strong. On the whole, the more regular pay and the general conditions of life in factories tended towards a higher standard of morals, although the critics of the factory system long denied it. As the new Century went on and factory pay and conditions steadily improved, the self-repsect of the women employed was put on a sounder economic basis.

The new age was bringing into being a large leisured class which had no direct relation either to the land, to the professions, to industry or to trade. In the years following the Napoleonic Wars there was much talk of the 'fund-holder,' who enjoyed incomes secured on the national credit.

Ever since the reign of William III, the constant increase in the funded National Debt with each new war was always expected to prove fatal to the country as the figures soared up decade after decade. But in fact the Debt never outran the increasing financial power of Britain, and the interest paid on it was nearly all spent within her four shores. At the beginning of George III's reign the 'fund-holders' had been reckoned at 17,000 persons, and about one-seventh of the total debt was at that time held abroad, largely by Dutch investors. But after Waterloo only a twenty-fifth part of Britain's now colossal debt was held by foreigners. In 1829 official statistics showed that the fund-holders numbered 275,839 persons, of whom more than 250,000 were small investors each receiving an annual interest of £200 or less.[1]

This meant a wide diffusion of safe and easily realizable wealth among a very great number of families. They were thrifty folk; in 1803 it had been calculated that a fifth of the interest paid by the State to its creditors was reinvested in the public funds. It is probable that most of the fund-holders were earning additional incomes in one way or another, but some were living inactive, respectable lives on their small, carefully treasured investments, particularly unmarried women, like the innocent ladies whom Mrs. Gaskell described in *Cranford*.

When Cobbett abused the 'fund-holders' as blood-suckers eating the taxes of the people, and demanded the repudiation of the National Debt, he hardly realized what an enormous number of inoffensive, humble folk he proposed to ruin, over and above

[1] Halévy, *Hist. of Eng. People* (Pelican ed.) II, pp. 204–212.

the 'stock-jobbers' who were perhaps fair game. Them he hated above all, partly because they helped to swell the 'wen' of greater London. The inexorable 'march of bricks and mortar,' burying for ever the green farmlands of Middlesex, was creating residential areas for the business men of the capital and for the stock-jobbers and fund-holders. With his heart in the old yeoman past of his country, Cobbett could not abide the sight of this new featureless swamp of houses, and this new artificial society with no roots in the soil. Yet of such towns and such people the England of the future would largely consist.

Brighton, famous for the patronage of George IV and for the Pavilion he had built there, was already an adjunct of London. [See § 29, 30.] 'Mark the process,' growled Cobbett; 'the town of Brighton, in Sussex, fifty miles from the wen, is on the seaside, and is thought by the stock-jobbers to afford a salubrious air. It is so situated that a coach which leaves it not very early in the morning, reaches London by noon. . . . Great parcels of stock-jobbers stay at Brighton, with the women and children. They skip backwards and forwards on the coaches and actually carry on stock-jobbing in Change Alley though they reside at Brighton.' (*Rural Rides*, May 5, 1823.)

During the first thirty years of the Century many changes in habits of life and thought were due to the steady infiltration of evangelical religion into all classes of society, finally not excepting the highest; it was a movement that spread from below upwards. An active individualist Protestantism, closely connected with humanitarian activity, strictness of personal conduct and avowed profession of piety had, as we have seen, been an important element in Eighteenth Century England, but had then exerted little influence on the latitudinarian Established Church or on the free lives of the enjoying classes. But when those classes saw their privileges and possessions threatened by Jacobin doctrines from across the Channel, a sharp revulsion from French 'atheism and deism' prepared a favourable soil for greater 'seriousness' among the gentry. Indifferentism and latitudinarianism in religion now seemed seditious and unpatriotic, and a concurrent change in manners took place, from licence or gaiety to hypocrisy or to virtue. Family prayers spread from the merchant's household to the dining-room of the country house. 'Sunday observance' was revived. 'It was a wonder to the lower orders,' wrote the *Annual Register* in 1798, 'throughout all parts of England, to see the avenues to the churches filled with carriages. This novel appearance prompted the simple country people to enquire what was the matter.'

If this change to religious seriousness had been nothing more than a symptom of the anti-Jacobin panic, it would have passed away with the passing of the danger. But it survived the return of peace in 1815, and came to terms with the liberal reaction that followed. The Victorian gentleman and his family were more religious in their habits and sober in their tone of thought than their predecessors in the light hearted days of Horace Walpole and Charles Fox. The English of all classes formed in the Nineteenth Century a strongly Protestant nation; most of them were religious, and most of them (including the Utilitarians and Agnostics) were 'serious,' with that strong preoccupation about morality which is the merit and danger of the Puritan character. In their double anxiety to obey a given ethical code and to 'get on' in profitable business, the typical men of the new age overlooked some of the other possibilities of life. An individualist commercialism and an equally individualist type of religion combined to produce a breed of self-reliant and reliable men, good citizens in many respects—but 'Philistines' in the phrase popularized by their most famous critic in a later generation. Neither machine industry nor evangelical religion had any use for art or beauty, which were despised as effeminate by the makers of the great factory towns of the North.

In the lower ranks of society, horror of French Republican atheism helped the Wesleyan movement to spread more widely than ever after the death of its great founder in 1791. Not only did the new Methodist Churches increase their membership to hundreds of thousands, but the methodist spirit was infused into older Nonconformist sects like the Baptists. On the eve of the French Revolution, the latitudinarian and radical spirit of Priestley and the Unitarians had to some extent penetrated other dissenting sects that were nominally orthodox. But that liberalizing influence was destroyed by the reaction with which the Century closed, and its place was taken by a strong, narrow evangelicalism. The various Nonconformist sects, thus reinspired to a fresh proselytizing activity, undertook the mission of Christianity in the new industrial districts, a task for which the Established Church at that time had neither the organization nor the zeal.

While the war lasted, the influence of the new type of Nonconformity was anti-French and on the whole conservative; the governing classes therefore regarded its increasing influence and numbers with less alarm than might otherwise have been felt. Common antipathy to Roman Catholics and to their reviving claim to civil equality, formed yet another link between the Tory upper class of the day and the Dissenting Sects under the new evangelical influence—to the chagrin of the aristocratic Whigs, in whom alone the broader Eighteenth Century attitude survived. But as soon as the war was over and anti-Jacobin fears had receded, the unreformed and highly privileged Church Establishment was left face to face with a number of powerful Nonconformist sects, all inspired by a new evangelical vigour, and no longer grateful for a bare toleration, like their feebler predecessors of a hundred years before.

The bridge between Establishment and Dissent, as also between anti-Jacobin and Liberal, was found in the small but influential Evangelical party which had now effected a lodgment inside the Church. Its ethos was not clerical like that of the Oxford Movement in the following generation. The most energetic among the Church clergy were indeed the Evangelicals, but they cared less about the Church as an institution than about the saving of souls, and they made no high claims on behalf of their own priesthood. Except Charles Simeon and Isaac Milner of Cambridge, the leading 'Saints' (as the Evangelicals were popularly called) were laymen —Wilberforce himself, the Buxtons and the Clapham 'Sect.' The strongest type of English gentleman in the new era was often evangelical. The army knew them with respect and India with fear and gratitude. Through families like the Stephens, their influence on Downing Street and on the permanent Civil Service and on Colonial administration was constantly increasing during the first forty years of the Century.

Humanitarian activity was the characteristic form in which their religious piety expressed itself. In the cause of the slaves they were ready to co-operate not only with their fellow Evangelicals, the Wesleyan and other Dissenters, but with free-thinkers and Utilitarians. Wilberforce confessed with chagrin that the 'high-and-dry' conservative party then prevalent among the Church

clergy obstructed the anti-Slavery cause or were at best indifferent, while Nonconformists and godless reformers proved
his staunchest allies. And the old free-thinker Bentham on his
side exclaimed: 'If to be an anti-slavist is to be a Saint, saintship
for me.' The same combination of forces—Church Evangelical,
Dissenter and free-thinking Radical—worked for the education
of the poor in the British and Foreign School Society, and in the
following generation for Shaftesbury's Factory legislation.

This cross-cut, traversing established party and denominational lines, indicated that the public mind was becoming more
active and independent. Many were now thinking and acting
for themselves, on subjects chosen by themselves, and were no
longer content merely to make a crowd at the hustings for the
benefit of the Whig or Tory aristocracy. This new power of
organized public opinion carried the abolition of the Slave Trade
in 1807, in the teeth of powerful vested interests, in the middle of
the anti-Jacobin reaction. The movement was not allowed to
drop after that first triumph, but was carried on to effect the
further object of freeing all the slaves in the British Empire;
Fowell Buxton in the 'twenties took on the leadership of this
cause, which triumphed in 1833, the year Wilberforce died.

Thus was Wilberforce rewarded for his complete honesty of
purpose. He had never shrunk from the pursuit of his great
humanitarian object even when after the French Revolution it
had become for a while extremely unpopular in the world of
politics and fashion; he had always been ready to work with persons of any party, class or religion who would support the cause.
He was an enthusiast who was always wise. He was an agitator
who always retained his powerful gift of social charm, the outcome of his sweet disposition. He is the classic example of the
use of the cross-bench politician in our two-party public life. He
could not have done what he did if he had desired office. With his
talents and position he would probably have been Pitt's successor
as Prime Minister if he had preferred party to mankind. His
sacrifice of one kind of fame and power gave him another and a
nobler title to remembrance.

The hold of Wilberforce and the anti-slavery movement on the
solid middle class in town and country was a thing entirely
beautiful—English of the best, and something new in the world.
For a whole generation, the anti-slavery champion was returned

at every election for the great popular constituency of Yorkshire. He could, if he himself had consented, have sat for it during the rest of his life. In those days, all the freeholders had to come up to the Cathedral city to vote. ' Boats are proceeding up the river (from Hull) heavily laden with voters,' says a letter in 1807, 'and hundreds are proceeding on foot.' 'Another large body, chiefly of the middle class, from Wensley Dale, was met on their road by one of the Committee. "For what parties, gentlemen, do you come?" "Wilberforce, to a man," was their leader's reply.' When on Sunday the vast floor of York Minster was packed with the freeholders of the three ridings, 'I was exactly reminded,' writes Wilberforce, 'of the great Jewish Passover in the Temple, in the reign of Josiah.'

Wilberforce and the anti-slavery men had introduced into English life and politics new methods of agitating and educating public opinion. The dissemination of facts and arguments; the answers to the mis-statements of the adversary on the pleasures of the 'Middle-passage' and the happiness of negro life in the plantations; the tracts; the subscriptions; the public meetings— all these methods of propaganda were systematized by methods familiar enough to-day but strange and new in that age. The quiet force of the Quakers was brought out of its long hibernation and launched into public life, taking the party politicians in flank. The methods of Wilberforce were afterwards imitated by the myriad leagues and societies—political, religious, philan-thropic and cultural—which have ever since been the arteries of English life. Public discussion and public agitation of every kind of question became the habit of the English people, very largely in imitation of Wilberforce's successful campaign. Voluntary association for every conceivable sort of purpose or cause became an integral part of English social life in the Nineteenth Century, filling up many of the gaps left by the limited scope of State action.

The British mercantile marine, which together with the Royal Navy thwarted the ambition of Bonaparte, was incomparably the greatest in the world. In the reign of George IV (1820–1830) its tonnage, close on two and a half millions, was still moved by wind and sail, though in 1821 steamers undertook the passenger service between Dover and Calais, reducing the passage to three

§23  Women weeding out the corn (1814)

§24 A modern Belle going to the Rooms at Bath

§25 Dr. Syntax with a Blue-stocking Beauty

§26 Dr. Syntax at a Card-Party

§27 Farmer Giles and his wife showing off their daughter Betty to their neighbours

§28 "The shop windows were filled with coloured cartoons"

§29  The Steyne at Brighton (1825)

530  The Yellow Room at the Pavilion, Brighton (1825)

§31 West India Docks, London

§32 The new midshipman dines with the captain

§33 "Turning in and out again"

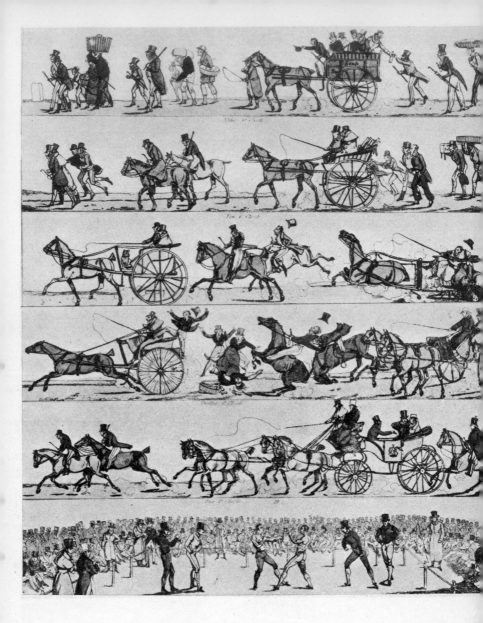

§34 "When the date and place of a prize-fight had been announced, hordes set out, driving, riding and walking to the spot from all parts of the island"

§35 Tom Cribb

§36 "The Ring" in 1821

§37 The Great St. Leger at Doncaster in 1825

§38 "Heroes of the Turf paying and receiving at Tattersall's" (after the St. Leger)

642. "Post chaises, gigs and dog carts racing each other and the coach."

§40 Inn yard at the "Bull and Mouth", London

§41 "The point of honour decided". A duel in Hyde Park

or four hours in favourable weather. By sea as well as land the age of steam was drawing near, though still in the future. But already engineering progress had transformed the approaches and harbours of the island. Between 1800 and 1830 Trinity House established lighthouses and floating lights round the coasts of England; docks were built in every considerable port town; the dock system of London was rapidly brought into being, though the 'Pool' was still thronged with tall masts in the river as far up as the bridge. [See § 31.] Pleasure piers, like those of Margate and Brighton, were also being built to attract the crowds of visitors to seaside resorts.

The Thames estuary still held unchallenged supremacy as the centre of Britain's trade and the World's. On the eve of the Reform Bill a quarter of the country's tonnage was owned and registered in London, including the great East Indiamen built for voyages of more than six months round the Cape to the India and China seas; Newcastle came next with 202,000 tons, chiefly coal ships, many of them to supply London; Liverpool came third with 162,000 tons, chiefly for the American trade; Sunderland and Whitehaven were fourth and fifth, dealing in coal along the East and West coasts respectively; Hull had 72,000; no other English port had over 50,000 tons. Clydeside had 84,000. (Clapham, *Ec. Hist. Modern Britain* I, pp. 3–8.)

The relation of the Royal Navy to the merchant marine and to the rest of the seagoing population—including fishermen, whalers and smugglers, was of the first importance in time of war. The link between the two was the chaotic and atrocious system of the press-gang. Some form of compulsion was required to man the fighting ships when they were put into commission, for conditions of life in the King's service were too bad to attract the required numbers of volunteers. But the method by which compulsion was applied was the worst possible. A proper register of seamen from whom conscripts might be taken in a just and orderly manner had been proposed by officials of the Admiralty during the wars against Louis XIV, but nothing had been done. The incompetence characteristic of State action and organization throughout the Eighteenth Century held good in this matter, even during the heroic age of the Navy. Still in the days of Nelson the press-gang was the terror of life along the coasts and in the harbours of England. Bands armed with cutlasses were led by the King's officers to crimp mariners and landsmen from ships in harbour or at sea, from ale-houses and streets, or even at the churchdoor whence bridegroom and congregation were sometimes carried off. Widespread injustice and misery were caused; families were ruined or broken up; and often very unsuitable recruits were obtained.[1]

Once on board the King's ship, the pressed man had too much reason to bemoan his fate. The food provided by swindling contractors was often disgusting, and the pay doled out by a penurious government was always insufficient. Improvement in these respects only followed as a consequence of the dangerous mutinies of Spithead and the Nore in 1797. Thereafter the sailor's lot was gradually improved, on lines that had been advocated for generations past by the best naval officers in their struggles with the authorities at home. Nelson's own relations to his men were a pattern of kindness. But it must stand on record that the common sailors who saved Britain at St. Vincent, Camperdown and the Nile, were many of them mutineers in the intervals of their magnificent service. The contrast between their grievances and their indiscipline on the one hand, and their splendid spirit in action and on the blockade service, may seem unaccountable. The explanation lay in this: the men before the mast knew that, for all the ill treatment they received, the nation regarded them as its bulwark and glory; that at the sight of one of Nelson's men with his tarry pig-tail, the landsman's eye kindled with affection and pride. The country that used them so ill, looked to them confidently to protect her, and they knew it. [See § 2.]

The naval officers, from among whom Nelson drew his 'band of brothers,' were more uniformly satisfactory than of old, though still occasionally quarrelsome and self-willed. In Stuart times the service had suffered from constant strife between the rough 'tarpaulin' captains of humble origin who knew the sea, and the fashionable landsmen sent from Court to share the command of the fleet. Those days had long gone by. The naval officers were now the sons of gentlemen of modest means (Nelson was a poor parson's son), sent to sea as boys, and combining what was best in the 'tarpaulin's' experience and training with the

---

[1] Mrs. Gaskell's *Sylvia's Lovers* gives a picture of Whitby about the year 1800, which throws much light on the ways of the press-gang, and on the English whalers of the Greenland and Arctic seas.

manner and thought of an educated man. [See § 32, 33.] Fanny's brother William, in *Mansfield Park*, and Captain Wentworth in *Persuasion* stand for all that was most attractive in the type. But there were all sorts of characters and idiosyncrasies among officers and men in the fleets of Nelson and Collingwood, which have been described by one of themselves in Captain Marryat's immortal *Peter Simple* and *Mr. Midshipman Easy.*

In the last few years of the struggle with Napoleon, the army became for a short time even more popular with the nation than the navy. The very completeness of victory at Trafalgar placed our 'storm-beaten ships' in the background of the war of which they remained the invisible support. It was now Wellington's victories that filled the minds of men. From 1812 to 1815, when the laurel-wreathed coaches cantered through village and market town bearing the news of Salamanca, Vittoria or Waterloo, the army became popular as it had never been before and never was again until the German Wars of the Twentieth Century, and then it was the nation itself in arms.

But Wellington's army was not the nation in arms, as was the conscript French army against which it fought. It consisted of aristocrats commanding privates taken from the lowest ranks of society, 'the scum of the earth' as Wellington declared them to be, though he added (as is often forgotten) 'it is really wonderful we should have made them the fine fellows they are' (Stanhope's *Conversations with the Duke of Wellington*, ed. 1889, pp. 14, 18.) The principal causes of enlistment were drink, unemployment, and personal trouble with a woman or with the laws of the land. The harsh discipline of the lash, considered necessary to keep such rough customers in order, served to prevent the more self-respecting members of society from joining the army as privates. In the earlier years of the Peninsular War the British soldiers plundered in spite of all Wellington's efforts, though never badly as the French whom Napoleon encouraged to live on the lands they conquered. But by the time our troops entered France in 1814, their discipline was excellent, and their self-respect and just pride as the best troops in Europe and the favourites of the folks at home was a credit to the odd social system on which the British army was based.

The military officers came from more aristocratic circles than the naval men. They were, many of them, like Wellington himself, cadets of the great families who led fashion and politics at home; others, like George Osborne in *Vanity Fair*, were of the wealthy bourgeoisie who could afford to buy their commissions and to mingle with the scions of the nobility. Between such officers and the men they led, the social gulf was immense and often resulted in gross neglect of the private soldier by officers too fashionable and sometimes too drunken to attend to their duty. The inefficiency and corruption of the army when the war began in 1793 was tested and exposed by the first campaigns in the Low Countries. A few years before, Cobbett, who had enlisted in the ranks and been promoted to sergeant-major, discovered that the Quarter-master of his regiment 'who had the issuing of the men's provision to them kept about a fourth part of it to himself,' and when Cobbett gallantly attempted to expose the scandal, he found that such proceedings were very generally connived at throughout the army; he fled to America to escape the vengeance of the authorities who would suffer no such prying into their methods and their perquisites.

As the long war went on, Sir Ralph Abercromby, Sir John Moore and Wellington gradually reformed this state of things; the British officer recovered his sense of duty and the army its discipline. But alike in the ill-managed and the well-managed regiments, the personal care and control of the privates was left to the sergeants, the 'non-commissioned officers,' who were indeed 'the backbone of the army.' The regiment was a society made up of grades answering to the social demarcations of the English village whence men and officers had come. It has been observed that when the ensign fresh from Eton was handed over to the respectful care and tuition of the colour-sergeant, the relation of the two closely resembled that to which the younger man had been accustomed at home, when the old gamekeeper took him out afield to teach him the management of his fowling-piece and the arts of approaching game.

There was no very strong professional feeling among the army officers of our most unmilitary nation. From the Duke downwards they hastened to get into mufti when off duty, though even the Duke was angry when some dandies in the Guards put up umbrellas to keep off the rain on the battlefield, as if it had been outside a club in St. James's Street! Only a few of the officers looked to the army as their real means of livelihood;

as such, indeed, it could not be very profitable, considering the price that had to be paid for commissions at each step in the service. It was a way of seeing life; of enjoying in Spain a sport even more exciting and arduous than big-game shooting; of making entry into the best society; of serving one's country in a manner suitable to one's youth. The Peninsular War produced a number of good English officers, and fostered a number of great regimental traditions, but it did not make an English military caste or an army organization of permanent value. When peace returned, most of the officers were willing enough to go home to the duties and pleasures of country-house life, to rural parsonages, or to the world of fashion and politics in town. England's army was not, like the army of France, of Spain and of Prussia, a military power rival to the civil power; it was a part-time occupation of some members of the governing aristocracy.[1]

During the long war two changes took place, indicating that at last the nation had accepted the standing army as a necessary national institution. At last barracks were built to house the troops, and the haphazard billeting of the soldiers on public houses came to an end, to the great relief both of the civilian population and of the soldiers themselves. At the same time the county militia ceased to be regarded as a line of defence, and was used as a source whence to supply the regular army with a reserve of trained recruits. The old idea that the defence of the island could be entrusted to the 'constitutional' militia of the shire, and that the 'standing army' was a dangerous temporary expedient, had been out of date for more than a hundred years, and now altogether passed away.

After Waterloo, a small standing army was maintained, but its popularity came to an end with the war. Though no longer regarded as a menace to the Constitution, it was regarded as an unnecessary expense by the economic anti-militarism of the new age. Moreover, the reformers now rising to influence disliked it as an aristocratic preserve. Such indeed it was; but the reformers, instead of proposing to reform it and democratize it, preferred to starve it and cut it down. Meanwhile the respectable working

[1] George Borrow's father, so well described in the opening chapters of *Lavengro*, was a fine example of the rarer type of officer who was not a man of fashion and to whom the army life was all in all.

classes continued to regard enlistment in the army as a sign of failure in life, if not of positive disgrace. Nineteenth Century England, having the good fortune to be safe from attack for several generations, conceived that so long as her navy was efficient her army could safely be neglected. And since it continued to be an aristocratic institution, it became increasingly unpopular with the rising democracy both of the middle and the working classes. It was regarded as a proof of British freedom that, unlike the other inhabitants of Europe, no man over here could be required to learn to defend his country in arms. This new and strange definition of liberty was

> The imposthume of much wealth and peace.

It became so ingrained during the hundred years of security that it proved very difficult to shake it off when danger returned in the Twentieth Century more formidably than ever before.

News of Wellington's campaigns in Spain was not awaited with greater national eagerness than reports on the prospects of famous horse-races and prize-fights. With the improvement of roads and communications, 'sporting events' ceased to be of purely local interest and became matters of intense concern to high and low in all parts of the country. Horse-racing indeed had flourished under royal patronage ever since Stuart times, but scientific pugilism had grown out of rude and vulgar beginnings in the reign of George II into the chief national interest in the Regency period. Just as the good-natured democracy of present-day England is well represented in the vast crowds of all classes, mingled together on terms of perfect equality, to watch a Test Match or a Cup Tie, so the more variegated social structure and rougher manners of that earlier time were best seen in the 'patronage' of 'the ring.'

When the date and place of a prize-fight had been announced, hordes set out, driving, riding and walking to the spot from all parts of the island. [See § 34.] Sometimes twenty thousand spectators assembled. In one aspect these vast outdoor assemblies were festivals of the common people. But the priests of the national cult were fashionable members of the aristocracy, who presided over the ceremonies and held the rough and often violent multitude in awe. It was these men of fashion and rank who hired

II   Clare Hall Piece and the New Buildings of King's, Cambridge

and backed the gladiators. Among those sturdy 'bruisers,' whose business it was to give and take 'punishment,' not a few ruffians could be found, but the real champions, men like Broughton, 'the father of British pugilism' in the reign of George II, and in the later times Belcher, Tom Cribb and Tom Spring were fine fellows and honourable men. [See § 35, 36.] Their lordly patrons were proud to be seen driving them to the ring-side in coach or gig. So too at race-meetings, the horses were owned by the men of fashion. Without aristocratic patronage sporting events would have lost half their zest and picturesqueness, and would very soon have degenerated into orgies of brutality and fraud, for the lower type of sporting men who surrounded the ring included too many like Thurtell, the murderer.

Indeed, with so much money wagered by the public, it was an uphill struggle for noble patrons to keep either the turf or the ring even comparatively honest. Without the moral jurisdiction of the fashionable Jockey Club, horse-racing would have become too disreputable to survive. [See § 37, 38.] That fate actually befell the prize-ring in the early days of Victoria, because 'cross' fighting and the sale of victories had become too common. The decline of prize-fighting was further hastened by the growing humanitarianism and religiosity of an age which forbade the setting on of animals to fight one another, and could scarcely do less for men. The recent revival of prize-fighting tempered with gloves, is more democratic, and largely American and cosmopolitan. It has not the peculiar tone of the English prize-ring in the days when handsome George was Regent and leader of fashion.[1]

When such was the most popular English sport, it can well be

---

The prize-ring in its 'most high and palmy state' was thus described by that soul of chivalry and honour, Lord Althorp, speaking in his old age to a friend: 'He said his conviction of the advantages of boxing was so strong that he had been seriously considering whether it was not a duty he owed to the public to go and attend every prize-fight which took place. In his opinion, cases of stabbing arose from the manly habit of boxing having been discouraged. He gave us an account of prize-fights he had attended, how he had seen Mendoza knocked down for the first five or six rounds by Humphreys and seeming almost beat, till the Jews got their money on; when a hint being given him, he began in earnest and soon turned the tables. He described a fight between Gully and the Chicken. How he rode down to Brickhill— how he was loitering about the inn door, when a barouche-and-four drove up with Lord Byron and a party, and Jackson the trainer—how they all dined together, and how pleasant it had been. Then the fight next day; the men stripping, the intense excitement, the sparring; then the first round, the attitude of the men it was really worthy of Homer.'

imagined that ordinary Englishmen were often at fisticuffs when they quarrelled, as readers of *Lavengro* and the *Pickwick Papers* are well aware. Indeed, young Dickens in 1836 could scarcely have drawn so popular a character as he meant Sam Weller to be, without endowing him with special gifts in knocking down his man.

As the century went on, when growing humanitarianism, evangelicalism and respectability helped to put down 'the ring,' they did the greater service of putting down the duel. The duel in the Eighteenth Century had been fought at push of rapier; in the early Nineteenth Century it was fought with pistols—like poor Rawdon Crawley's 'same which I shot Captain Marker.' [See § 41.] As the spirit of the age became less aristocratic and more bourgeois, less military and more completely civilian and more 'seriously' religious and, let us say at once, more sensible, duelling gradually dropped out. But the change had only begun by the time of the Reform Bill. Statesmen still quarrelled and fought with political opponents or rivals. In 1829, Wellington, then Prime Minister, being an old-fashioned fellow, thought it necessary to call out Lord Winchilsea and have a shot at him. Pitt, too, had exchanged shots with Tierney, and Canning with Castlereagh; but in Victoria's reign Prime Ministers and other gentlemen were restrained, by a changed code of public morals, from vindicating their honour by a method so absurd.

These early years of the Century saw the culmination of a delightful popular art, the 'coloured print.' It ruled the mind and imagination of the age, as photography and the film rule ours. The shop windows were filled with 'coloured cartoons,' fiercely political and libellously personal, glowing with the genius of Gillray or the no less vigorous social comedy of Rowlandson. [See § 28.] Other favourite themes, illustrated in a more conventionally heroic style, were the battles of the Peninsula, and incidents in the wars of all Europe, as far as the Russian snows strewn with frozen Frenchmen, or sea-pieces of our ships engaging the enemy. In quieter colours, Ackermann's beautiful prints showed the homely dignity of Oxford and Cambridge Colleges. [See Plate II.]

But above all, the coloured prints represented the outdoor world of sport, from big-game shooting in India and Africa to the field-sports and the life of the road at home. [See § 44.] It is through these sporting prints, still treasured and often reproduced, that our generation best knows the spirit of that bygone epoch. Through them we are still familiar with the bustle of the galleried inn-yard when the coaches were starting, the young swell seated in the expensive place of honour beside the mail-coachman on the box, the heavy middle-aged men of business well wrapped up on the seats behind, the red-coated guard in rear of all [see § 40] ; then the scene on the open road, the post-chaises, gigs and dog-carts racing each other and the coach, over Macadam's hard, smooth surface [see § 39]; the adventure when the travellers are held up by flood or snow. Then the shooters in their top hats approaching the partridges that their dogs have pointed in the stubble [see § 43]; the spaniels flushing the cock pheasants out of the brushwood; the hardy sportsman wading through ice and snow after geese, wild duck and swan. Last, but not least, the hounds in full cry, and the career of the red-coated hunt, to whom the countryside, recently enclosed and drained, presents with its new hedges and channelled watercourses the cheerful aspect of innumerable 'jumps.' [See Plate I.]

There was no luxury about the field sports of those days. Hard exercise and spartan habits were the condition of all pursuit of game. This devotion took the leaders of the English world out of doors and helped to inspire the class that then set the mode in everything from poetry to pugilism, with an intimate love and knowledge of woodland, hedgerow and moor, and a strong preference for country over town life which is too seldom found in the leaders of fashion in any age or land.

Indirectly, therefore, the passion for shooting game did much for what was best in our civilization. But it was unfortunately connected with the poaching war and all manner of unneighbourliness. The legislation affecting 'game' was exclusive and selfish not only towards the poor but towards everyone except an aristocratic few. It was illegal for anyone to buy or sell game—with the result that prices obtainable by professional poachers were much increased; and it was illegal for anyone who was not a squire or a squire's eldest son to kill game even at the invitation of the owner. This inconvenient law could indeed be evaded by a process known as 'deputation.' And it was abolished by the Whig legislators of 1831, in spite of the opposition of the Duke of

Wellington, who was convinced that these extraordinary restrictions were the only means of keeping game in the countryside, just as he thought that the rotten boroughs were the only way of keeping gentlemen in politics. In both cases the event proved that he was too pessimistic.

By a new law of 1816, the starving cottager who went out to take a hare or rabbit for the family pot could be transported for seven years if caught with his nets upon him at night. [See § 42.] Less sympathy need be felt for the bands of armed ruffians from the towns who invaded the preserves and fought pitched battles, twenty a side, with shot-guns at close range, against the gentlemen and gamekeepers who came out against them. The poaching war had become a very ugly business.

One of its worst features was the protection of pheasant preserves by hiding mantraps and spring-guns in the brushwood, thereby maiming and killing innocent wanderers quite as often as the poachers for whom the engines of death were intended. The English judges pronounced the infamous practice to be legal, until Parliament put it under the ban of the law by an Act of 1827. The humanitarian spirit was beginning to be too strong even for the zealots of game preservation, against whom it then proceeded to win a long series of victories in the matter of the game laws. As those laws became milder and were more justly executed, the preservation of game became less difficult as well as less scandalous.

Indeed as the Nineteenth Century advanced and as the anti-Jacobin spirit receded, humanitarianism invaded one province of life after another, softening the rude and often brutal temper of the past, and fostering instead a cheerful benevolence of heart sometimes running to sentimentality. The destined prophet of this new phase of popular feeling in its strength and its weakness, was Charles Dickens, who grew to sensitive manhood in the hard school of London streets in the 'twenties. During that decade the 'bloody code' of death penalties for innumerable offences was being repealed, under pressure from juries who often refused to convict a man for theft if he was to be hanged for it. The age of Eldon was passing, the age of Bentham and Brougham was coming in. The movement for the abolition of negro slavery aroused passionate popular enthusiasm sometimes excessive in its sentiment for the 'dusky brother.'

These changes of feeling were a striking improvement upon all past ages. As the Nineteenth Century grew older, humanity pervaded more and more all the dealings of life, particularly the treatment of children. The advance in humanity, far more than the boasted advance in machinery, was the thing of which the Nineteenth Century had best reason to be proud; for in the wrong hands machinery may destroy humanity.

## Chapter Three

## BETWEEN THE TWO REFORM BILLS, 1832–1867

THE interval between the Great Reform Bill of 1832 and the end of the Nineteenth Century may, if we like, be called the Victorian Age, but it was characterized by such constant and rapid change in economic circumstance, social custom and intellectual atmosphere, that we must not think of these seventy years as having a fixed likeness one to another, merely because more than sixty of them were presided over by 'the Queen' (1837–1901). If any real unity is to be ascribed to the Victorian era in England, it must be found in two governing conditions: first, there was no great war and no fear of catastrophe from without; and secondly, the whole period was marked by interest in religious questions and was deeply influenced by seriousness of thought and self-discipline of character, an outcome of the Puritan ethos. This 'seriousness' affected even the 'agnostics' who, in the last part of the period, challenged not the ethics but the dogmas of Christianity, with increasing success on account of Darwinism and the discoveries of science. Moreover, the High Church movement, originated by Evangelicals who had seen a new light, inherited this strain of Puritanism. Mr. Gladstone, an Anglo-Catholic of that breed, appealed to the heart of his Nonconformist followers, because both orator and audience regarded life (including politics and foreign policy) as a branch of personal religion. [See § 100.]

Throughout the last seventy years of the Nineteenth Century the State was rapidly undertaking new social functions, rendered necessary by new industrial conditions in an overcrowded island; but the real strength and felicity of the Victorian age lay less in that circumstance, important as it was, than in the self-discipline and self-reliance of the individual Englishman, derived indeed from many sources, but to a large extent sprung from Puritan traditions to which the Wesleyan and Evangelical movements had given another lease of life. 'Self-help' was a favourite motto with leading and characteristic men in all classes. In the

Twentieth Century, on the other hand, self-discipline and self-reliance are somewhat less in evidence, and a quasi-religious demand for social salvation through State action has taken the place of older and more personal creeds. Science has undermined the old forms of religious belief, but even now the strength and the weakness of England cannot be understood without some knowledge of her religious history. In the twenty years between the two German wars (1919–1939) the moral idea, though less influential on personal conduct, was still expected, by the emancipated descendants of the Victorian religionists, to dictate our foreign policies and our disarmament, with all too little regard to actualities in other European nations who had never been Puritan, and had never regarded morals as having anything to do with policy.

During the period of the Napoleonic Wars and the first decade of peace that followed, the Evangelical clergy had become an integral part of the Church Establishment, to which they brought a vitality and enthusiasm that was still lacking in its other sections. The life's work of Charles Simeon (1759–1836), Fellow of King's and Minister of Holy Trinity Church, Cambridge, had done much to reconcile the proselytizing fervour of Evangelicalism to the discipline of the Church. Had it not been for Simeon, the evangelical clergy would have continued to drift into Dissent, as the easier method of conducting a peripatetic mission after the manner of Wesley, athwart the bounds of the parish system and in defiance of Church order. If this movement had continued in the new Century the Church of England might perhaps have fallen when the tempest of 'Reform' blew high in the 'thirties. But the Simeonite clergy, though friendly to Dissenters, effectively defended the Church whose mission to souls they did so much to revive.[1]

Except for the Evangelicals, the Church under the Regency remained very much as it had been in the early years of George III; only its latitudinarian liberalism had hardened into anti-Jacobin orthodoxy, unaccompanied by any spiritual awakening except what was supplied by the Simeonite leaven. Still, as in the Eighteenth Century, the clergy of the Establishment were sharply divided into rich and poor. The Bishops, the Cathedral

---

[1] *Simeon and Church Order*, Canon Charles Smyth's Birkbeck Lectures, Cam. Press, 1940.

CHURCH REFORM
'Gallop among the Bishops'
(*Enquiry into the income of Bishops*)

clergy and wealthier parish priests were part of the 'enjoying' class; they had obtained preferment not as a reward of work done for the Church, but through aristocratic connection or family favour. The parishes were often perfunctorily served or were left to the ministration of underpaid curates and threadbare incumbents of poor livings, who were not in the circle visited by the manor-house or acknowledged by Lady Catherine de Bourgh. All this had been highly congenial to the Eighteenth Century, when a 'place' in Church or State was regarded not as a solemn public trust but as a coveted prize. But in the new Age of Reform, opinion began to demand that a man should do the work for which he was paid. Every institution, from the 'rotten borough' to the Church benefice, was subjected to the rude Benthamite enquiry: 'What is the use of it?'

Moreover, the clergy of the Establishment were unpopular because they adhered, more faithfully than any other class or profession, to the High Tory party in the day of its decline and downfall. The formidable hosts of Nonconformists and of free-thinking Radicals, though loving each other little, united to attack ecclesiastical privilege. Young intellectuals, like John Sterling at Cambridge in 1826, described the parson in every village as 'a black dragoon,' kept there to do battle for the powers of tyranny and obscurantism.

Another and perhaps more just description of the well-connected parson as village autocrat at this period may be quoted from Dean Church. (*The Oxford Movement*, pp. 4, 10.)

When communication was so difficult and infrequent, he filled a place in the country life of England, that no one else could fill. He was often the patriarch of his parish, its ruler, its doctor, its lawyer, its magistrate, as well as its teacher, before whom vice trembled and rebellion dared not show itself. The idea of the priest was not quite forgotten; but there was much—much even of good and useful—to obscure it.

Dean Church also recalls the type of 'country gentlemen in orders, who rode to hounds, and shot and danced and farmed, and often

CHURCH REFORM
'Mother Church putting her own house in order'
(*Payment of poor clergy*)

did worse things,' and the 'pluralists who built fortunes and endowed families out of the Church.'

Under these general conditions, it is not wonderful that the Radical Press, in lampoons, articles and gross caricatures of plump red-faced eaters of tithe, attacked the Anglican clergy more fiercely than they had been attacked since the days of the Long Parliament. Their unpopularity came to a head in 1831, when the Spiritual Peers in the House of Lords voted by twenty-one to two against the Reform Bill. That winter, the Reform mobs took a special delight in stoning the coaches and burning the palaces of Bishops.

Trembling churchmen and their exultant enemies both assumed that the first work of the reformed Parliament of 1833 would be to remedy the admitted grievances of the Dissenters and that before very long the Church would be disestablished and disendowed. 'No human means are likely to avert the threatened overthrow of the Establishment,' wrote the Tory Southey. 'The Church as it now is, no human power can save,' wrote Dr. Arnold of Rugby, the Liberal-Conservative. But a Century has since gone by, and the Establishment, though shorn of its Irish and Welsh excrescences, maintains its endowments and its connection with the State, scarcely any longer challenged. Even the removal of the most obvious grievances of the Dissenters, instead of being carried at a rush in the first decade after the Reform Bill, was spread over fifty years.

The threatened ecclesiastical revolution was side-tracked, and the chief causes of the unpopularity of the Church were done away by friendly hands. Parliament reformed the unequal distribution of clerical wealth, and there was a rapid revival of religious activity among the clergy themselves, which evoked a rally of the laity to defend the Church and to participate in its parochial work.

The Parliamentary measures necessary for Church reform were carried out by the co-operation of the Conservative leader Peel with the Whig statesmen. The men of the new Oxford Movement protested against the interference of the State with ecclesiastical revenues, but no other machinery existed to effect these necessary changes, and the wiser members of the Episcopal Bench, like Blomfield, co-operated with Whig and Tory statesmen in the work of the Ecclesiastical Commission and the Acts

§42 The poacher's family plead his pardon before the scuire (1817)

§43 Partridge shooting

§44 Hog Hunters meeting by surprise a tigress and her cubs

§45 Harrow Schoolroom

§46 Cricket at Rugby

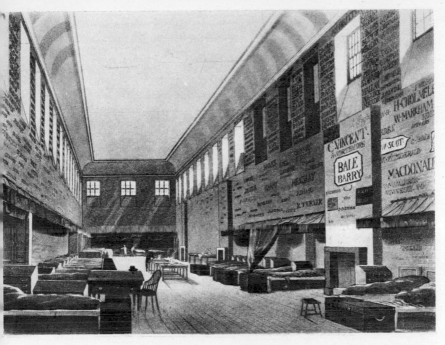

§47 Dormitory at Westminster

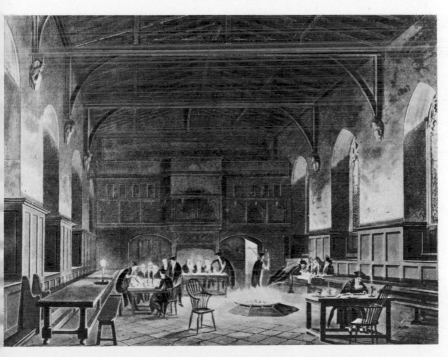

§48 Refectory of the King's Scholars, Westminster

§49 Dr. Thomas Arnol.

§50 John Stuart Mill

§51 Thomas Carlyle

§52 John Ruskin

§53 "Appropriate situations for residences" (1841)

§54 The old castle at Balmoral

§55 "The deer that the Prince shot and Landseer painted".
Prince Albert at Balmoral by Landseer

§56 Balmoral as rebuilt for Queen Victoria

§57 Prince Albert's study at Balmoral

§58 "He pulls his mansion down to show his taste" (1817)

§59 A villa in Regent's Park (1828)

§60 Mid-Victorian suburban villas at Hackney

§61 A Gloucestershire clergyman's house (1857)

§63 "Castle". Gothic. Goodrich Court, Herefordshire (built 1828–31)

§64 London University (founded 1827)

§65 The University Museum, Oxford (1855).
"The first-fruits of Ruskin's teaching in Oxford"

of Parliament which were passed on its advice between 1836 and 1840.

These Acts removed the worst abuses in the distribution of endowments, and partially at least bridged the gap between rich and poor clergy—though not completely, as readers of Trollope's novels will remember. Plurality was restricted by law, members of chapters being forbidden to hold more than one benefice or to belong to more than one chapter. The Cathedral clergy were reduced in numbers and in wealth. By such measures one hundred and thirty thousand pounds a year were saved and were applied to raise the stipends of the poorer parsons and curates. The diocesan boundaries were altered, and the Bishoprics of Manchester and Ripon were created to cope with the new industrial population of the North. The great inequalities in episcopal revenues were remedied, and scandalously large incomes cut down.

As a consequence of these reforms the Church was no longer assailed as a part of ' old Corruption.' Radical cartoons ceased to represent Bishops, deans and prebendaries as fat, worldly, rapacious men, living on the sweat of the poor.

At the same time the Church, under the inspiration of the spirit of the age, began to supplement by her own action the mediaeval geography of the parish system. New parishes were created, and churches were built in industrial districts, till then abandoned to the activity of the Nonconformists, or to no religion at all. Bishop Blomfield raised a great fund for building churches in outer London. For there was no longer any question of obtaining new churches out of public funds. Tory Parliaments had voted taxes to build churches in Anne's reign, and again after Waterloo. But after 1832 no government dared propose to mulct the taxpayer for such a purpose.

It was difficult to preserve the fabric even of the existing churches by forcing parishioners to pay the Church Rate, which continued for another generation to be a subject of fierce local controversy wherever the Dissenters were strong, especially in the industrial districts of the North. At Rochdale in 1840, when a poll was being taken to decide whether or not a Church Rate should be levied, passion ran so high that troops were drafted into the town to keep order with fixed bayonets.

For all further development and new undertakings, the

Church had therefore to rely on raising money by voluntary subscription, as the Free Churches had always done. And the maintenance of the Anglican Schools, at that time the principal part of the primary education of the country, depended almost entirely on voluntary contribution.

The Whig government also relieved the Church of the worst unpopularity of the tithe system, which from time immemorial had caused heart-burning not only to Dissenters but to the whole agricultural community. The harvest song—

> We've cheated the parson, we'll cheat him again,
> For why should the Vicar have one in ten?

expressed a sentiment as old as Anglo-Saxon England. The tithe was levied from the tenant farmer, very often in kind: the tenth sucking-pig went to the parson's table; the tenth sheaf was carried off to his tithe barn. Long before the Reformation it had been a cause of friction and bitterness. Chaucer had praised the good parson who did not 'cursen for his tithes,' that is, excommunicate the recalcitrant tithe-payer.

The Tithe Commutation Act of 1836 laid this ancient grievance to rest. It stopped payment in kind. Tithes were commuted for a rent-charge on land. In 1891 it was made payable by the landowner, no longer by the tenant farmer except perhaps indirectly through his rent. The squires, who were socially and politically allied to the parsons, did not object to paying tithe as strongly as their tenants. The Commutation Acts gave peace to the countryside. It was only in our own day, when after 1918 so many cultivating farmers bought their own land and having become landowners found themselves directly chargeable with tithe, that a fresh agitation arose leading to fresh concessions at the expense of the Church.

Another grievance was remedied by the Marriage Act of 1836. By Lord Hardwicke's Marriage Act of 1753, no one could be legally married except by a Church of England parson, an intolerable insult to the religious feelings of Protestant Dissenters and still more of Roman Catholics. The Act of 1836 permitted religious ceremonies in Catholic or Protestant dissenting places of worship, that should be legally binding if notified to the Registrar. For the Act established civil officers called Registrars of Births, Deaths and Marriages—in itself a notable reform consonant with the new era of statistics and exact information. Religious marriage in the Church of England was left as before, on condition that the parson sent to the Civil Registrar a duplicate of the entry of marriage made in the Vestry. This typical English compromise between the modern secular State and the old religious world is still the law of the land.

These various reforms saved the Church from the serious attack upon her that had been predicted alike by friend and foe. Nevertheless, political and social divisions remained very largely religious. The leading Conservatives in each town and village were usually the keenest churchmen, while their most active opponents, Whig and Liberal, were Dissenters or Anti-clericals. The lower-middle and working classes attended the same chapels and took part in the same religious activities. Politics in the Nineteenth Century were as much a matter of denomination as of class. The religious cleavage running through society was maintained all the more because the Whigs after 1832 failed to remedy the Dissenters' grievances about Church Rates, Burials and admission to Oxford and Cambridge. For a long time to come England was less 'class-conscious' than 'church-and-chapel conscious.'

In the more old-fashioned parts of England—let us say in 'Barsetshire'—the clergy were still under the patronage and influence of the upper class. But in other parts of England many now served parishes where there were few or none of the higher orders of society, owing to the geographic segregation of classes which the Industrial Revolution was bringing about. The 'slum parson' came into being, a man with a different set of ideas and functions from those of the clerical autocrat of the old English village.

The internal vigour of Church life in the middle decades of the Nineteenth Century was derived from a variety of sources. The average parson of no particular school of thought was aware that he must bestir himself in a critical age. The specifically evangelical influence was much more widely diffused and fashionable in Church circles than in the early years of the century: the 'low Churchmen,' as the Evangelicals were now called, were strong enough to enforce, both by law and custom, more 'Sabbath observance' than in the previous easy-going age. And at the same time, the Anglo-Catholic ideal, emanating from the Oxford of the 'thirties and 'forties, gradually spread its thoughts and practices throughout the land. In each of these aspects, the ecclesiastical picture of the Church of the 'fifties and 'sixties is well known to readers of Trollope's 'Barsetshire' novels. In shires less remote, there was also the 'broad church' school of Frederick Denison

SUNDAY OBSERVANCE
'Puritan Sunday or what we must all come to'

Maurice and Charles Kingsley, called 'Christian socialist' because of its interest in working-class life and education, derived in part from the exhortations of Thomas Carlyle, himself no churchman. The Broad Church school was never strong in numbers, but its ways of thought came to have influence on many more orthodox clergymen, though at first both its 'heresies' and its 'socialism' had been regarded with grave reprobation. Thus the Church of England, not without many invigorating controversies and vain attempts to expel either ritualism or heresy, became the multiform body to which we are now so well accustomed, liberally receptive of many different ways of life and thought.

After Newman's conversion to Rome in 1845, the Oxford Movement, which he had done so much to originate, divided itself into two separate currents. One, guided by Pusey and Keble,

'Please, Mr. Bishop, which is Popery and which is Puseyism?'

continued to promote the Anglo-Catholic cause in the established Church,[1] The other, led by Newman and later by Manning, stimulated the revival of the long depressed Roman Catholic mission in England. Having been accorded the status of civic

[1] 'Anglo-Catholicism' was a novelty in the early Nineteenth Century, but it was not new in the longer range of Anglican History. The Laudian clergy perhaps, and the Nonjurors certainly, might have been called 'Anglo-Catholics': the Oxford Tractarians resembled the Nonjurors, *minus* their Jacobitism. Two Irish Churchmen, Bishop Jebb and Alexander Knox, had also adumbrated Anglo-catholic principles a generation before the Oxford Movement gave them a national importance. The ritualistic side of Anglo-Catholic services only developed as the Century went on: it was not a marked feature of the original Oxford Movement.

equality by the Catholic Emancipation Act of 1829, and being perpetually recruited by Irish immigration into England, the Roman community went on increasing in numbers and influence.

Popular outburst against 'Papal aggression.' 'A Prospect of Exeter Hall showinge a Christian Gentleman Denouncynge ye Pope'

But in 1850 it was still obnoxious to a strongly Protestant nation, as was shown by the misdirected popular outburst against the so-called 'Papal aggression,' when the Pope set up territorial Bishops in England.

Meanwhile the Nonconformist strength went on increasing, as the middle and working classes of the new industrial order continued to grow in numbers, wealth, political power and social esteem. In the 'sixties, when Matthew Arnold held up an unflattering mirror to the bloated face of English society, it was above all the Nonconformist 'Philistines' whom his Oxford soul abhorred; he saw in them the representative men of their generation, proud of their old English liberties and their new-gotten wealth, but with too little other idea of the social and intellectual needs of a community deficient in 'sweetness and light.' But many of these wealthier industrialists of the new order joined the more fashionable Established Church, and passed into the ranks of the upper class by self-assertion or by marriage. 'Society was getting mixed.'

Another poet, Robert Browning, not of Oxford, perceived better what strength and comfort was added by Puritan religion to the lives of the poor and the hardworking orders of society. And, indeed, to judge from Matthew Arnold's sonnet *East London*, he too sometimes understood.[1]

The enormously increased wealth and manufacturing power of England in the first half of Victoria's reign—the

> Mammon-quakings dire as earth's—

and their twin progeny, a new middle class without tradition and a raw industrial proletariat, needed a corresponding development of education to fructify and enlighten them. Unfortunately no government before Gladstone's in 1870 dared to evoke the battle of rival denominations which was certain to ensue from any proposal for State Education, when Church and Dissent would assuredly fly at one another's throats over the question of religious teaching. In 1841 Sir James Graham wrote to Brougham: 'Religion, the keystone of education, is in this country the bar to its progress.' All that the timid State ventured to do,

> Between the pass and fell incensed points
> Of mighty opposites,

was to make a grant of twenty thousand pounds a year towards the school buildings of the various voluntary societies. This was begun in 1833 and the meagre allowance was annually renewed. To distribute this pittance, an Educational Committee of the Privy Council was set up, with a permanent Secretary and a system of inspection of the State-aided schools. Such was the humble origin of the present Ministry of Education. The insistence on government inspection as a condition of a government grant was a principle destined ere long to dominate many spheres of life. The Factory inspectors, set up by the Factory Act of 1833,

---

[1] William Law Mathieson, *English Church Reform 1815-40*; Dean Church, *The Oxford Movement*; *Pretractarian Oxford* by W. Tuckwell; Matthew Arnold, *Culture and Anarchy*.

bred School Inspectors; Mine Inspectors shortly followed. Government inspection was on the march; the time would come when it would affect half the activities of the land.

Meanwhile, twenty thousand pounds a year was not much for the richest State in the world to spend on education. The Prussian State was educating the whole Prussian people. The paternal rulers of Germany in the early Nineteenth Century educated their subjects, but gave them little political freedom and no share in government. The English State gave the common people great political freedom and some share in government, but left them to be educated by private religious charity. Only after the working classes of the towns had been enfranchised by the Reform Act of 1867, did the politicians at last say: 'We must educate our masters.'

While such was the inadequate provision for the primary education of the masses, secondary education of the well-to-do underwent a remarkable development in the growth of the 'Public School system.'

At the beginning of the Century there were three kinds of secondary schools: the fashionable 'Public Schools' (really private) like Eton, Winchester and Harrow, still few in number, with a purely classical curriculum and shockingly ill disciplined; secondly, the private Academies, where the unfashionable Dissenting middle class received a more scientific and modern education under better discipline; and finally the old endowed Grammar Schools, many of which had decayed through the negligence and corruption characteristic of public institutions in the Eighteenth Century.

With the growth of the power and wealth of England and the need for every kind of leadership at home and oversea that the new Century demanded, a great increase of secondary education was essential. And it was to some extent supplied, but in an unexpected way that had important social consequences. It might have been supposed that the age of Reform and the approach of democracy would lead to the improvement and multiplication of endowed Grammar Schools by State action; in that case a common education would have been shared by the clever children of very various classes, as had been done in the Grammar Schools of Tudor and Stuart times with such excellent results. But in the Victorian era the Grammar Schools remained less important, in spite of some striking exceptions as at Manchester. At the same time the Dissenting Academies, so useful in the previous century, petered out. The new fashion was all for the 'Public School,' modelled on the old ideals of Eton, Westminster, Winchester and Harrow, of which Rugby became the great exemplar. [See § 45, 46, 47, 48.]

This development was partly due to chance, in the advent of a single man. The great educational reformer of the 'thirties was Dr. Thomas Arnold, Head Master of Rugby. [See § 49.] His emphasis on religion and the chapel services, his monitorial system and his largely successful attempt to suppress bullying, drinking, profligacy and the worst indiscipline of the old 'bear-garden' type of Public School, set an example that proved infectious. The old establishments were reformed and others were started in eager competition. 'Organized games,' which Arnold himself had by no means over-emphasized, grew up automatically, dominating and further popularizing Public School life, and spreading in due course to Oxford and Cambridge.[1]

The 'middling orders of society' found in the reformed Public School the door of entrance for their sons into the 'governing class.' The old landed gentry, the professional men and the new industrialists were educated together, forming an enlarged and modernized aristocracy, sufficiently numerous to meet the various needs of government and of leadership in Victoria's England and Victoria's Empire.

In many respects the Public Schools were a success and filled the part required. But the subjects which they taught were too much confined to the Classics to meet all the requirements of the new age, though they formed the basis for a high development

---

[1] How much reason careful and pious parents had to dread the influence on their sons of the Public School before the period of 'Arnold' reforms and the growth of organized games, can be read in Cowper's *Tirocinium* (1785):

> Would you your son should be a sot or dunce,
> Lascivious, headstrong, or all these at once;
> Train him in public with a mob of boys,
> Childish in mischief only and in noise,
> Else of a mannish growth, and five in ten
> In infidelity and lewdness men.
> There shall he learn, ere sixteen winters old
> That authors are most useful pawned or sold;
> That pedantry is all that schools impart
> But taverns teach the knowledge of the heart.

The whole poem is worth the attention of the student of social history.

of literary culture at Oxford and Cambridge, and in Tennyson's England at large. In the microcosm of 'public school' life, wherein the boys were left to form and govern their own society, character gained more than originality, and intellect was less encouraged than sturdy schoolboy faithfulness to comrades. Twenty and more years after Dr. Arnold's death, his critical son Matthew called the English governing class 'barbarians': the Public Schools had tended to preserve both the virtues and the limitations of 'earth's primitive, vigorous sons.'

The upper, the upper-middle and the professional classes were welded together in the Public Schools, and by the same process were further divided from the rest of the nation brought up under a different educational system. The tendency to social segregation, enhanced by the geographic division of the various class 'quarters' in the lay-out of great modern cities, was thus further accentuated by education. Moreover, the expenses of a Public School, so much higher than those of the Grammar School and Day School, became a terrible self-imposed burden on middle-class and professional families. Indeed, at the end of the Century it became a principal cause of the lamentable decrease in the number of children in some of the best sections of the community.

Much of the success and much of the failure of modern England can be attributed to the Public Schools. They were one of the great institutions unconsciously developed by English instinct and character, and even less than Parliaments could they be successfully imitated oversea.

In the middle years of the Century the secondary education of girls was very ill provided for. They were sacrificed to pay for the expensive education of their brothers. In that and in other matters concerning women, the great emancipation and improvement was postponed till the last thirty years of Victoria's reign—the real period of the 'emancipation of women' in England.

Yet in spite of Matthew Arnold's pert and challenging phraseology about upper-class 'barbarians' and middle-class 'Philistines,' he himself was a prophet and poet of the age he abused, and in spite of his scorn for our system of secondary education as 'the worst in the world,' the fact remains that the higher culture of Nineteenth Century England was varied, solid and widespread over a large proportion of the community. The world is not likely to see again so fine and broad a culture for many centuries to come.

Already in the middle years of the Nineteenth Century, industrial change was creating the mass-vulgarity which was destined ere long to swamp that high standard of literary culture with the advent of the new journalism, the decay of the country-side, and the mechanization of life. Scientific education, when at last it came, inevitably displaced humanism. But in the mid-Nineteenth Century, education was still humanistic not scientific, and though this had some serious practical disadvantages, it made for the time being a great literary civilization, based on scholarship, with an even wider following of intelligent readers than in the Eighteenth Century, and with a much more varied and catholic scope in style and matter than in the days when Boileau and Pope were the standards of taste. In literature and thought as well as in society and politics it was an age of transition from aristocracy to democracy, from authority to mass-judgment; and for literature and thought such conditions were propitious, so long as they lasted.

Serious historical works were addressed to a very wide public and hit their mark, by no means in the case of Macaulay alone. The atmosphere of free religious controversy, of moral reflection, of anxious and reverent doubts on orthodox creeds and the search for a substitute, gave body and interest to imaginative writers like Carlyle, Ruskin and the author of *In Memoriam* and made Wordsworth in his old age more popular than Byron in his grave. [See § 51, 52.] At the same time the critical analysis of actual society, perceived to be very faulty and believed to be remediable, helped to inspire and to popularize Dickens, Thackeray, Mrs. Gaskell and Trollope. [See § 66, 67.] And the rights of personality, even in the case of women, were represented in the writings of the Brontë sisters no less than in the life's work of Florence Nightingale. John Stuart Mill on *Liberty* (1859) and on the *Subjection of Women* (1869) attacked the bondage of convention and proclaimed the rights of individual men and women to free life and thought, in a manner that may be taken as a turning-point between the early and the later Victorian age. [See § 50.]

The aspect of science which is nearest akin to humanism, the close and loving interpretation of nature, was another source that inspired the literature of the time and another cause of its wide appeal. In the later Eighteenth Century, the way had been prepared by White of Selborne, Bewick and other naturalists both professional and amateur, who taught their countrymen to observe and reverence the world of nature, in which it was man's privilege to dwell. At the turn of the Century this widespread habit found further expression in the landscapes of Girtin, Turner and Constable, and in the poetry of Wordsworth and Keats. In the following generation, in the 'thirties, 'forties and 'fifties, de Wint, David Cox, Edward Lear and many others were added to the list of landscape painters of real talent, who could not even in water-colour paint fast enough to satisfy the public demand. And in poetry the long reign of Tennyson covered most of the Victorian era. His strongest appeal lay in the strength, beauty and accuracy of his pictures of nature. [See § 98.]

Indeed, Tennyson, when at his best, was able to clothe the accurate observation of natural objects with 'the light that never was on sea or land.' That commended him to the Victorians, who were susceptible both to the magic of words and the loveliness of nature. The more precise pictures that Tennyson's poetry evoked displaced the vaguer nature-scenes of Thomson's *Seasons*, which until his advent had retained the affections of the middle-class reading public. Early in Victoria's reign the ladies of *Cranford* were told about Tennyson: 'This young man comes and tells me that ash buds are black; and I look and they *are* black.'

Very similar was the source of Ruskin's influence over the same reading public, which sprang up suddenly in the 'forties and continued for many years. In *Modern Painters*, written to advocate the claims of English landscape painting, particularly that of Turner, and later to defend the Pre-Raphaelites, he analysed in prose at once lucid and magnificent the beauty of form in clouds, mountains and vegetation—the work of God spread wide for the delight of man. He may have erred in testing the value of pictures overmuch by their approximation to truth in these respects, but he gave new eyes to his countrymen in their journeys to the Alps and to Italy, and in their walks in their own familiar woods and fields.

Europe, then a world of comparative peace and variegated beauty, not yet mechanized and not yet closed by war and national hatred, was the great playground of the English, who

III   Queen Victoria's sitting room at Balmoral

flocked abroad in thousands to spend their newly gotten wealth in exploring the mountains and flower-meadows of Switzerland, the architecture, the galleries, and the landscapes of the Netherlands, Italy and France. The English traveller of this period took abroad a full mind equipped by some knowledge of history, literature and natural science to observe and appreciate the glory of the world of nature and of man. [See § 70, 71, 72, 73, 74.]

At the same time the new railway system of Britain opened out the Highlands of Scotland to pedestrians and tourists with a zeal for mountain air and scenery. The wealthier and more fashionable had their deer-forest or their grouse-moor where they entertained their guests every autumn. The moorland expeditions of the Queen and Prince Albert from Balmoral, and the deer that the Prince shot and Landseer painted, popularized Highland scenery with all classes of the English, who were now able to see the landscape of Scott's romances for themselves. [See § 54, 55, 56, 57.]

Thus, in the middle years of the Century, Victoria's subjects developed eyes for many kinds of natural beauty and historical interest. [See § 53.] They enjoyed a great literary civilization, both in reading the classics of the past and producing classics of their own age. But these grandfathers and great-grandfathers of ours, though they compassed sea and land to admire Roman aqueducts and Gothic Cathedrals, themselves produced deplorable buildings, and filled them with appropriate furniture and knick-knacks. In these respects the decay of taste between the period of the Regency and the period of the Prince Consort was astonishing. [See Plate III and see § 58, 59, 60, 61, 62, 63.] The most refined and educated classes were as bad as any: the monstrosities of architecture erected by order of the Dons of Oxford and Cambridge Colleges in the days of William Butterfield and Alfred Waterhouse give daily pain to posterity.

An unfortunate habit of the time was the demolition of beautiful old manor-houses of manageable size, to make room for ugly rural palaces where the rich men of Britain's most prosperous era entertained their troops of guests from London. Their descendants, with better taste in architecture and with less money in the Bank, have reason to regret the burdens thus bequeathed them.

It is not altogether easy to account for this architectural blind spot in the Victorian vision. But Ruskin, as chief priest, was in part responsible, in that he condemned, on fantastic religious grounds, the whole Renaissance tradition, of which real English

'Ye Exhybityon at ye Royal Academye'

architecture was essentially a part. [See § 65.] His influence filtered down through society till it reached people who never read a line of his books, and jerry-builders believed that if they 'stuck on a bit of Gothic ornament,' all was well. The real secret of architecture, proportion, was lost. At bottom the Industrial Revolution was to blame: the mechanization of building and other trades, and the decline of craftsmanship were no doubt the deep underlying causes. Local customs in architecture, based on the use of local materials, were destroyed by the railways, which supplied standardized cheap bricks and slates, to take the place of local stone, stone-tiles, thatch and thin brick, which previous generations of countrymen had known how to use aright by inherited skill and regional tradition. But now building everywhere became a process of cheap mass-production of houses by modern methods. [See § 69.] New furniture, machine-made, was as bad. The fat upholstered arm-chairs might be more comfortable, the new houses might be more convenient, but beauty spread her wings and flew away.

In the 'forties, 'fifties and 'sixties painting was still a great trade, supplying a great demand. For the photographer had not yet sufficiently developed his science to take the place of the painter's art in the production of family portraits, copies of famous pictures and representations of ancient buildings and favourite landscapes. At Rome, and in every artistic capital of Europe, resided an army of artists, good and bad, painting landscapes and copying 'old masters' to sell to the touring English, who carried back these mementoes of their travels. [See § 72.] And the Royal Academy was in its heyday, commercially speaking, supplying the rising manufacturers with portraits, landscapes and historical pieces—to cover the large walls of their comfortable, new, pretentious homes. It was partly because this trade was so extensive that Ruskin became so important. He exercised over art the kind of dictatorship which the *Edinburgh* and *Quarterly* reviews had formerly exercised over literature. The complaint of the demoded R.A. was thus parodied:

> I paints and paints,
> Hears no complaints,
> And sells before I'm dry;
> Till savage Ruskin
> Sticks his tusk in
> And nobody will buy.

The same dangers from the same combination of religious and social forces, which in the years immediately preceding the Reform Bill had threatened the clergy of the Establishment, threatened also the old Municipal Corporations with which the Church interest was allied.[1] But unlike the Church, the old Corporations were as incapable of recovery or self-reform as the Parliamentary Rotten Boroughs with which their fate was closely associated. Three years after the death of the 'Rotten Boroughs,' the rotten Town governments were abolished by the Municipal Reform Act of 1835.

[1] Light on this alliance is thrown in the article entitled *A Leicester Election of 1826* in the *Royal Historical Society Transactions* for 1940. See also Halévy's *Hist. of Eng. People* (Ernest Benn, Watkin's transl. 1927), III, pp. 217–220.

That important measure meant much to the social life of cities, by the immediate transference of power to new classes; and it meant more than was then foreseen, as the basis on which was to arise, during the next hundred years, the great structure of municipal social service for the benefit of all classes of the community, particularly of the poor. No one in 1835 foresaw the day when the 'new municipalities' would not only light and pave the streets, but control the building of houses, and the sanitation and health of the borough; convey the workmen to and from their work; provide public libraries; carry on great municipal trades and industries; and finally educate the people.

The immediate change that excited contemporaries was the transference of municipal authority, such as it then was, to Dissenters and shopkeepers, in place of the co-optive oligarchies of Tory lawyers, Churchmen and noblemen's agents who had enjoyed a close monopoly of the old corporations. There was not much 'sweetness and light' in the new style of city governor, but they had a certain rough vigour, and were disposed to welcome 'improvements,' while the fact that they were periodically chosen by a real democracy, kept them up to the mark in those matters in which the electors themselves felt any interest. The limitation of the Parliamentary franchise to 'ten pound householders' in the Reform Bill of 1832 was not imitated in the more radical Municipal Reform Bill, which gave the local franchise to all ratepayers. The working class had a say at least in local elections in the new Boroughs. The town administration thus passed into entirely new hands; moreover, the judicial bench of magistrates in large urban areas was filled up by the Whig governments, acting on behalf of the Crown, with Dissenters and middle-class citizens of the newly dominant types. There were to be no more 'Peterloo magistrates' in the cities of England.

The Reform Bill of 1832 and its sequel in the Municipal Reform Bill of 1835, taken together, emphasized and increased the differentiation between the social life of town and country which economic forces were every day making more complete. Victoria's England consisted of two strongly contrasted social systems, the aristocratic England of the rural districts and the democratic England of the great cities. The counties and the market towns were still ruled and judged by country gentlemen to whom all classes bowed. But the cities were governed by a

§66 Charles Dickens

§67 W. M. Thackeray

§68 Air view of a Yorkshire woollen mill (showing gradual industrial growth in a rural area)

§69 Air view of "back-to-back" houses in Burnley, Lancs., showing 19th-century industrial housing

§70 The Great Briton in the Rhineland

§71 The English "milord" upon Rhine

§72 At the Academy in Venice

§73 Descent of the St. Gotthard in a diligence

§74 Relaxation on the Grand Canal in Venice

§75 "A Court for King Cholera"
—slums behind Oxford St.,
London, in 1864

§76 Going to the Great Exhibition in 1851

§77 The Great Exhibition

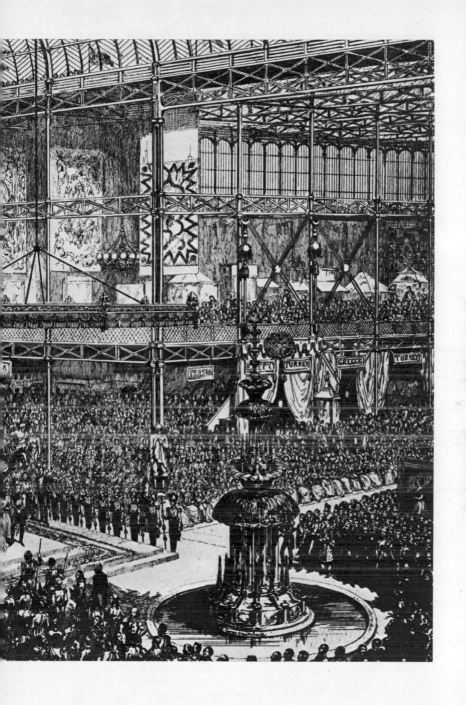

§78 Hyde Park in 1842

§79  Marble Arch in 1857

§81  River traffic by Lambeth Palace in 1857

§82 The Course

§83 Carriages and child performer

§84 Soldiers leaving for the East, 1857

totally different type of person in accordance with a very different scale of social values which, whether middle or working class, were essentially democratic.

Owing to economic causes and the progress of locomotion, the new society of the town was perpetually encroaching on the old society of the country till, in the Twentieth Century, urban thought, ideas and government conquered the countryside itself. [See § 68.] But that was a long process and the Nineteenth Century was an age of transition. Agriculture was not at once ruined by the Repeal of the Corn Laws in 1846, nor was aristocratic government of the villages and market towns overthrown by that measure. Until the American prairies were able to empty their grain and cattle into the English market a generation later, English agriculture flourished, sustaining the social system with which it was associated.

But agriculture was not capable of indefinite expansion; by the middle of the Century it had reached its highest development and the acreage of land could not be increased. On the other hand, the Industrial and Commercial Revolution was only then gathering its full strength, and the increase of town wealth and population went on decade after decade. The Census of 1851 showed that already half the population of the island was urban, 'a situation that had probably not existed before, in a great country, at any time in the world's history.' (Clapham, I, p. 536.) And since there was no visible limit to this process, it was ominous of a queer future. John Bull was ceasing to be a countryman and a farmer; when once he was wholly urbanized or suburbanized, would he any longer be John Bull, except in the cartoons of *Punch*?

The new urban conditions, under which so large a proportion of the English people were already living in 1851, began at length to attract attention and demand a remedy. The old life of the open countryside, blown through by the airs of heaven, needed, or was thought to need, less control of housing and sanitation: bad as rural cottages were, the death-rate was lower in the country than in the town. But owing to the increased proportion of town dwellers, the rapid fall of the death-rate that had so happily distinguished the period between 1780 and 1810 was positively checked between 1810 and 1850. Taking the island as a whole, the death-rate did not again rise as high as in the early part of the Eighteenth Century, but it ceased to decline any further, in spite of the constant advance in medical service and science. (See Vol. 3 p. 40.) The chief reason was the growth of the area covered by industrial slums, and their progressive deterioration as years went by.

In the matter of guardianship of public health, the rule of shopkeepers, builders and publicans, elected by the ratepayers under the Municipal Reform Act of 1835, was no real improvement on the lethargy of the Tory oligarchs who had been displaced amid such general rejoicings. Still throughout the 'forties nothing was done to control the slum-landlords and jerry-builders who, according to the prevalent *laissez-faire* philosophy, were engaged from motives of self-interest in forwarding the general happiness. These pioneers of 'progress' saved space by crowding families into single rooms or thrusting them underground into cellars, and saved money by the use of cheap and insufficient building material, and by providing no drains—or, worse still, by providing drains that oozed into the water-supply. [See § 75.] In London, Lord Shaftesbury discovered a room with a family in each of its four corners, and a room with a cesspool immediately below its boarded floor. We may even regard it as fortunate that cholera ensued, first in the year of the Reform Bill and then in 1848, because the sensational character of this novel visitation scared society into the tardy beginnings of sanitary self-defence. A full-page cartoon in the most popular journal of the time represents Mr. Punch as Hamlet in meditation over a City sewer—'Why may not imagination trace the remains of an Alderman till we find them poisoning his Ward?'

The first Public Health Act dates from 1848. It resulted from the cholera and from the efforts of Edwin Chadwick, who as Secretary to the Poor Law Commissioners had come to realize the facts.

The prisons [he wrote] were formerly distinguished for their filth and bad ventilation; but the descriptions given by Howard of the worst prisons he visited in England (which he states were among the worst he had seen in Europe) were exceeded in every wynd in Edinburgh and Glasgow inspected by Dr. Arnott and myself. More filth, worse physical suffering and moral disorder than Howard describes are to be found amongst the cellar populations of the working people of Liverpool, Manchester or Leeds and in large portions of the Metropolis.

But the Public Health Act of 1848 of which the main principle was permission rather than compulsion to act, was not properly carried out by the municipalities for another twenty years. It was only in the 'seventies that the establishment of the Local Government Board to enforce the law, and the rise of Joseph Chamberlain the social-reforming Mayor of Birmingham, ushered in a new age. Then at last the fact that the Municipalities were elected bodies produced real public benefits on a large scale, while the State increasingly insisted on a compulsory standard. Not till the 'seventies did the death-rate decisively fall as a result of building and sanitary reform, and not till the end of the Century was sanitation in English cities at all what it should have been.

But even in the middle years of the Century slight improvement had been made. Lord Shaftesbury had, by voluntary subscriptions, established some model lodging houses, and their immunity from cholera induced Parliament to pass an Act for the inspection of common lodging houses in 1851; at the same time the window tax, that old enemy of health and light, was at last repealed. In that year, when the Great Exhibition spread its hospitable glass roof high over the elms of Hyde Park, and all the world came to admire England's wealth, progress and enlightenment, an ' exhibition' might profitably have been made of the way in which our poor were housed, to teach the admiring foreign visitor some of the dangers that beset the path of the vaunted new era. [See § 76, 77.] Foreign slums were indeed many of them as bad or worse, but a much smaller proportion of the populations of Continental States had been removed from the wholesome influence of the countryside.

If we ask why those who sympathized with the victims of a lopsided 'Political Economy' called it the 'dismal science,' we get some answer in the following unctuous passage from the *Economist* newspaper, written in May 1848 in opposition to Chadwick's Public Health Act:

Suffering and evil are nature's admonitions; they cannot be got rid of; and the impatient attempts of benevolence to banish them from the world by legislation, before benevolence has learnt their object and their end, have always been more productive of evil than good.

Doctrine of one kind or another has been the cause of half the woes of mankind, but fortunately the English of this period were not entirely doctrinaires, and passed the Ten Hours Bill and the Public Health Act in despite of the prevalent *laissez-faire* theories of the age.[1]

Meanwhile, if public health still lagged behind, public order had been well secured. Sir Robert Peel's great institution of the civilian police with their truncheons, blue coats and top hats (later exchanged for helmets) had only applied to the Metropolitan area in 1829. But a people fond of liberty, property and personal safety liked the good-natured and effective 'Bobbies' of London and demanded their establishment elsewhere. By 1856 every county and borough had to employ a police force, half local, half national in its administration, discipline and finance. The days of the inefficient Watchman of the Dogberry and Verges type were gone by for ever; person and property were well guarded at last without any sacrifice of freedom, and mobs and meetings could be dealt with, punctually and quietly, without calling on armed force as at Peterloo.

The period between the two first Reform Bills (1832–1867) was the 'age of coal and iron' now working at full blast, or in other words it was 'the Railway Age.'

The railways were England's gift to the world. They originated from experiments in the best method of moving coal from the pit-head in the vast quantities required for smelting and manufacture as well as for domestic use. In the 'twenties there had been much controversy as to the rival merits of drawing coal along wooden or iron rails by horses, or by stationary engines, or by George Stephenson's 'locomotive.' The triumph of the latter opened out unexpected vistas not only for the carriage of all classes of goods but as a new method of passenger traffic. [See § 85.] Not only the canals but the stage-coaches were doomed; Mr. Weller senior's occupation was gone. Short local lines laid down in the coal districts were developed in the 'thirties and 'forties into a national system for the whole island, as a result of two distinct periods of railway investment

---

[1] Clapham, I, pp. 536–547; Fay, C. R., *Great Britain from Adam Smith to the present day*, pp. 362–365; *Ec. Hist. Rev.*, Ap. 1935, pp. 71–78; Griffith, *Population problems of the age of Malthus*, pp. 39–42.

and speculation, in 1836–1837 and in 1844–1848. [See § 86, 87, 88, 89.]

Many of the railroad promoters and investors who led the

'A Railway Station. Showynge ye Travellers Refreshynge themselves'

way in the 'thirties were Dissenters, and more particularly Quakers of the Midlands and the North—Peases, Croppers, Sturges. The original *Bradshaw's Railway Time Table* was issued in 1839 by a Friend wishful to help mankind; until the Twentieth Century the outside cover of 'Bradshaw' still bore the Quaker's designation of the month—'First Month' instead of January, and so forth.

But in the 'forties, under the less scrupulous leadership of George Hudson, the 'Railway King,' the general public plunged headlong into the speculation of the 'railway mania,' and lost much money in bogus or unsuccessful companies. Thackeray's Diary of *Jeames de la Pluche, Esq.*, humorously chronicles the excitement of the boom and the crash. But when all was over, though the more foolish part of the public had been gulled, a large residuum of successful new lines survived. Hudson was not a mere swindler; he had scored his mark across the face of England. In 1843 there had been about 2000 miles of railway in Great Britain; in 1848 there were 5000.[1]

Henceforth the normal way of transporting heavy goods and the normal way of long-distance travelling was by rail. The canals, after half a century of prosperity and public service, were most of them ruined, and were many of them bought up by local railway companies that had in fact been started with the object of cutting them out. At the same time the main roads ceased to be the chief arteries of the life-blood of the nation. The posting inns and postilions disappeared, and with them went the public mail-coach, and the heavy family coach in which the aristocratic households had moved about. In the Capital, the convenient 'landau,' the light 'Victoria,' the smart 'hansom cab' (called by Disraeli 'the gondola of London'), the homely four-wheeler and the democratic omnibus held the streets. [See Plate IV and § 78, 79, 80, 81.] In the country at large it was the age of the gig, the wagonette, the pony-cart and the dog-cart. Horse-traffic, both for travellers and for goods, became ancillary to the railway and flourished on that basis. There were not railways everywhere and in any case it was necessary to 'get to the station.' Byroads continued to increase in number, quality and use. But long journeys by road went out, and the great highways were relatively deserted, until the coming of the motor car.[2]

The growth of the electric telegraph was almost contemporaneous with the change in locomotion, and originated as an adjunct of the new railway system. By 1848 over 1800 miles of railways, a third of the whole mileage in use, were already equipped with telegraph wires. The Electric Telegraph Company, formed in 1846, had seventeen offices in London by 1854, of which eight were at the railway termini. As early as 1847 arrangements for the candidature of the Prince Consort for the

[1]Sir Roger Scatcherd, in Trollope's *Dr. Thorne*, represents a 'self-made man' of this rough vigorous period of railway and engineering development carried out by English initiative at home and abroad. For the autobiography of a real engineer of the period, of a more respectable type than the imaginary Scatcherd, see *John Brunton's Book*, Cam. Press, 1939.

[2] Seymour's well-known illustration of the row with the cabman in Chap. II of *Pickwick* shows the aboriginal form of the 'hansom cab' in the 'thirties, with the driving-seat not above but at the side of the high roof. From the 'forties onwards changes in locomotion, dress, games and social customs can be followed in the pictures of *Punch*.

Chancellorship of the University were in part conducted by telegram, even by such old-fashioned people as the dons of Cambridge.

Rowland Hill's Triumphal Entry into St. Martin's-le-Grand

The same decades that saw the rapid growth of the railway system and the electric telegraph, saw the triumph of the penny post, established by the unselfish and tireless efforts of Rowland Hill, supported by the popular demand, against the indifference of statesmen and the angry obstruction of the unreformed civil service. Prior to this great change, the poor who moved in search of work either inside the island or by emigration overseas, could seldom exchange news with the parents and friends they had left behind, owing to the heavy charge made for the receipt of letters. Rowland Hill's plan for a postal delivery prepaid by a

71

cheap adhesive stamp, enabled the poor, for the first time in the history of man, to communicate with the loved ones from whom they were separated. And since the business world found cheap postage a boon, and since it proved a great financial success after it had been forced upon the obdurate Post Office, the new method was soon imitated in every civilized country in the world. In this great reform the State had necessarily to be made the instrument, but the thought and the leadership had come from an individual, backed by public opinion.

The rapid growth of railways in the island during the 'forties was followed by the substitution of steam for sail, and of iron for wood in the British mercantile marine. As late as 1847 our steamships were few and small, with a total tonnage of 116,000 out of the three million tons of the whole merchant service. But in the 'fifties and 'sixties the great ocean-going ships were increasingly propelled by steam, and built first of iron and then of steel. The change coincided with the enormous development of English iron and steel output, and the increased use of steam and metal in every sort of manufacturing process and product. In 1848 Britain already produced about half the pig-iron of the world: in the next thirty years her output was trebled. The West of Scotland, hitherto behindhand, was soon producing a quarter of Britain's pig-iron. Staffordshire, Wales and the North-Eastern England of Tyneside and Middlesbrough were also the regions of the great ironmasters, who by due attention to scientific discovery carried on their supremacy into the age of steel.[1]

The wealth accruing from these developments in the mid-Victorian era greatly relieved the pressure of the social problem by raising the real wages of a large proportion of the working class, while Trade Union action and the Co-operative movement helped to distribute the enormous national dividend a little more evenly.

The national dividend was indeed enormous. The Californian and Australian gold discoveries ushered in a great period of expanding trade of which England, by her lead over other countries both in commerce and industry, was able to reap the

---

[1] Clapham (II, 515) points out that in Petermann's census map of the location of industries in 1851, neither Middlesbrough nor Barrow, neither Cardiff nor Newport are marked as the seat of iron industry. Their rise as such was very rapid after that date.

principal benefit in the middle years of the Century. In 1870 the volume of the external trade of the United Kingdom exceeded that of France, Germany and Italy together and was between three and four times that of the United States.

The Gold Rush. The Road Sweeper off to California

While these great industrial and commercial developments were going forward at revolutionary speed, British agriculture continued along a steady path of progress, helped by abundance of capital and the increasing application of machinery to farm work. The Repeal of the Corn Laws in 1846 steadied prices, but gave no check to agricultural prosperity for another generation to come, because America was not yet ready to flood England with her farm products. In 1851 it was reckoned that only one quarter of the Englishman's bread came from oversea.

Corn Law Repeal was a political triumph for Manchester and for the urban population; and it certainly helped industry. But it effected no immediate economic or social revolution. The

cities belonged to democracy, but the countryside was still in the
hands of the landlord class, and of their deputies and allies the
tenant farmers, whose affairs were much more flourishing in the
'sixties than they had been a generation before. Country-house
life, with its hunting and shooting, and its political and literary
'house-parties' was more prosperous, easy and delightful than
ever, though its moral standards were more 'respectable' than
in the days of Eighteenth Century aristocratic licence. In the
rural parts there was still no elective local government. Administrative and judicial authority still rested with the gentlemen
Justices of the Peace, chosen from among the landowners. The
immemorial rule of the squire magistrate still prevailed, though
subject, through the newspapers and the spirit of the age, to a
more wholesome and effective criticism than in the early
Hanoverian times.

With locomotion constantly diminishing the distance between
the village and the city, with the spread of science and machinery
even in the processes of agriculture, in a small island with a dense
urban population that had now lost all tradition of country life,
it was only a question of time before urban ways of thought and
action would penetrate and absorb the old rural world, obliterat-
ing its distinctive features and local variations. But the time was
not yet. In the 'sixties two things were still lacking before the
change could be complete—the economic ruin of British
agriculture, and a town-made system of universal education.

When Victoria came to the throne the ' great estate' system
was already an accomplished fact. Ever since the days of the last
Stuart Kings, more and more land had been passing from small
squires and cultivating owners into the possession of the big
landlords, into whose circle the men of the new town-made
wealth were constantly intruding themselves by marriage, by the
purchase of large continuous estates, and by the building of new
'country houses.' The small squires had gone, their manor-houses
converted into tenant farms; the freehold yeomen were fewer
than of old; large and middle-sized estates were the general rule.

But if estates were large, it did not follow that farms had proportionately increased in size. On the average they were bigger
than before. But moderate-sized farms worked by a single
family without hired labour were still very common. And indeed

IV    Bus interior in 1859

such farms are very numerous even to-day, especially in the pastoral counties of the North, the more so as machinery has reduced the number of hands required.[1]

So far was land from falling out of cultivation during the two decades following the Repeal of the Corn Laws in 1846, that more and more acres were enclosed and cultivated. [See § 91.] There was a constant increase of the island population, that had still to be fed mainly by home produce. The gold discoveries of the 'fifties raised prices. In the 'sixties, while wars raged in Europe and in America, England was at peace. Great progress was still being made in live-stock breeding. Improved draining and manuring; the gradual introduction of machine ploughing, reaping and threshing into one county and village after another; the work of the Royal Agricultural Society; the capital invested and the pride taken by the great landlords in the improvement of their estates—all these things brought more fields under the plough in Lord Palmerston's England. When Matthew Arnold revisited in the 'sixties the Oxford hillsides where he had strayed with his friend Arthur Clough twenty years before, it was not yet 'bungaloid growth' that the poet had to bemoan, but the more innocent spread of cultivation!

> I know these slopes; who knows them if not I?—
>> But many a dingle on the loved hillside,
>>> With thorns once studded, old, white-blossomed trees,
> Where thick the cowslips grew, and far descried
>> High towered the spikes of purple orchises,
>>> Hath since our day put by
> The coronals of that forgotten time;
>> *Down each green bank hath gone the ploughboy's team,*
>> And only in the hidden brookside gleam
> Primroses, orphans of the flowery prime.

---

[1] In 1851, omitting holdings under 5 acres, the size of farms in England and Wales was thus scheduled:

| Size—acres | No. of farms | Acreage of group |
|---|---|---|
| 1.    5–49 | 90,100 | 2,122,800 |
| 2.    50–99 | 44,600 | 3,206,500 |
| 3.    100–299 | 64,200 | 11,015,800 |
| 4.    300–499 | 11,600 | 4,360,000 |
| 5.    500–999 | 4,300 | 2,841,000 |
| 6.    1000 and upwards | 771 | 1,112,300 |

Clapham, *Ec. Hist. of Modern Britain*, II, p. 264.

At Victoria's accession, the enclosure of the 'open fields' and therewith the end of the 'strip' system of agriculture, was already an accomplished fact, except for a few scattered survivals. But

'A Banquet Showynge ye Farmers Friend impressynge on ye
Agricultural interest that it is ruined'

the enclosure of commons was not yet complete and still went on apace, stimulated by the General Enclosure Act of 1845.

The movement for the enclosure of common land—for so many centuries past a source of disputes and grievances, as well as a means of greatly increasing the productivity of the island—was halted at last in the decade between 1865 and 1875. It was characteristic of the altered balance of society that enclosure of commons was ultimately stopped by the protest not of the rural peasantry, but of the urban population, who objected to exclusion from its holiday playgrounds and rural breathing spaces. The Commons Preservation Society effectively opposed the destruction of the remaining commons, in the interest, nominally and legally, of the vanishing 'commoner' of the village, but really of the general public in quest of 'air and exercise.' The great battle of

Berkhamsted Common (1866) and the saving of Epping Forest ushered in a new age. Enclosure had done its work in England, and was to do no more. (*Clapham*, I, 450 note, 454; II, 258-9.)

The prosperous agriculture of the eighteen-sixties still showed a great variety of method, from the fully mechanized farming of scientific Scots in the Lothians, to fields in Sussex where oxen still dragged the plough. Those lands that had been enclosed during the last two hundred years from open field, sheep-run and fen into large rectangular fields, were most easily subject to modern scientific and mechanical cultivation, as for instance in Cambridgeshire. Lands of the West and South-East, where enclosure had existed from time immemorial, were still cut up by old hedges into small and irregular fields that impeded agricultural efficiency. But in almost every shire there was much diversity of method, due either to variety of soils or difference in the economic and social past.

The condition of the agricultural labourer, particularly in the South, was often very wretched in the 'thirties and 'hungry 'forties,' when even the farmer who employed him was suffering from the bad times. [See § 90.] And on the 'labouring poor,' in field and factory, fell the heavy weight of the New Poor Law of 1834, when outdoor relief was abolished (not indeed quite universally) and the 'workhouse test' was imposed on applicants for public alms. Such was the remorseless utilitarian logic of the Poor Law Commissioners, to whom the Act gave power. It was a harsh remedy for a terrible disease: the Speenhamland policy of granting the poor-rate in aid of wages had pauperized even the employed workman and kept wages down; moreover, it was now ruining the ratepayers. (See p. 7.) An operation was necessary to save society, but the knife was applied without anaesthetics. The need to make life in the workhouse less attractive than employment in field and factory was the principle on which the Commissioners worked, and as they could not in that era raise the attractiveness of employment by enforcing a minimum wage, they felt obliged to lower the standard of happiness of the workhouse. Moreover, in their preoccupation with the problem of the adult workman, the Commissions overlooked the justice and expediency of treating old people, children and invalids with the tenderness that was in every sense their due.

Dickens's *Oliver Twist* was an attack on workhouse management, to which the greater sensibility of the Victorian public responded. The working class in town and country regarded the New Poor Law as an odious tyranny, as indeed it often was. But it had created a central machine which, by displacing the old local autonomy, was used as years went by to remedy the grievances of the poor and to make a national system of which the country had less reason to be ashamed. The national and centralized character which the first Commissioners had stamped on the Poor Law made it easier to carry out the many improvements suggested later on by a philanthropy that gradually became more humane as it became more experienced and more scientific. Imperfect and harsh as was the Poor Law in 1834, it had been intellectually honest within its limits, and contained the seeds of its own reform.

For the system erected for the new Poor Law was based not on *laissez-faire* but on its opposite. It was pure Benthamism, a combination of the elective with the bureaucratic principle, as advocated in Bentham's 'Constitutional Code.' The three government Commissioners (bureaucrats representing the Central government) are to lay down the rules for poor law administration and to see they are enforced. But the actual people to administer these rules are local elective bodies—the boards of guardians. Every 'union' of parishes is to be administered by a 'board of guardians of the poor,' to be elected by all the ratepayers. Both the centralized bureaucrats at the top, and the democratically elected Boards of guardians in the localities, are the Benthamite substitute for the old methods of government by country gentlemen acting as unpaid Justices of the Peace.

But the new Poor Law of 1834 was a very unfortunate beginning for reformed methods of governing the countryside. Its harshness, especially in the separation of families,[1] gave the

[1] In 1838 the popular writer William Howitt in his *Rural life of England* (II, p. 131), after describing the simple pleasures of country life for the cottager, adds: 'I often thank God that the poor have their objects of admiration and attraction; their domestic affections and their family ties, out of which spring a thousand simple and substantial pleasures; that in this country at least the hand of arbitrary power dare seldom enter this enchanted circle, and tear asunder husband from wife, parent from children, brother from sister, as it does in the lands of slavery. Yet our New Poor Laws have aimed a deadly blow at this blessed security. And, till the sound feeling of the nation shall have again disarmed them of this fearful authority, every poor man's family is liable, on the occurrence of some chance stroke of destitution, to have to their misfortune, bitter enough in itself, added the tenfold aggravation of being torn asunder and immured in the separate wards of a Poverty Prison.'

rural poor a distaste for Benthamite improvement, and reconciled them to the old paternal government of the Justices of Peace in all other matters, which went on for another fifty years. The New Poor Law might have served as a model for other changes in local government, but it was too unpopular.

Why did the Whig and Tory squires acquiesce in this encroachment on their right to rule the countryside, in this one matter of poor law administration? It was only in the case of the Poor Law that they allowed State bureaucracy and electoral democracy to invade the rural parts. The reason is clear. The country gentlemen had a direct interest in the change. Under the old system of rates in aid of wages, the poor rate which they paid was growing heavier every year, and pessimists prophesied that it would finally absorb the entire rent of the kingdom. The Whig Ministers had presented the Bill as 'a measure of agricultural relief,' and Peel and Wellington accepted it as such. At Wellington's orders, the Lords resisted the temptation to throw out this very unpopular measure.

With the increasing prosperity of industry and agriculture in the 'fifties and 'sixties, the lot of the wage-earner in town and country was greatly relieved. Shortly after 1870 agricultural wages had reached a point that they were never again to touch for many years. All along, in bad times and good, the wages of the field worker in the North were higher than in the South owing to the neighbourhood of coal-mines and higher paid industries. Agricultural Wages in the West Riding of Yorkshire had been fourteen shillings a week when they were seven shillings in Wilts and Suffolk. (Clapham, I, pp. 466–467; II, p. 286, table.)

The labourer, driven off the enclosed common and open field, had sometimes found compensation in allotments and potato-patches provided for him by philanthropic squires, parsons and farmers. The potato was of great service to the field labourer in the Nineteenth Century. But the allotment movement went slowly, and was no more than an occasional palliative.

In the 'fifties and 'sixties, while agriculture still flourished, good brick cottages, with slate roofs and two or even three bedrooms apiece, were being built by landlords as 'estate cottages,' particularly on large estates like those of the Duke of Bedford. The bad cottages were the old ones, of which there were plenty, built of mud, lath and plaster, and roofed with ill-repaired thatch, with only two rooms to the whole cottage. 'The worst were generally the small freeholds, inhabited by the person who owned them.' The farmhouses were not only larger but on the average more habitable than the cottages. The best had usually been erected recently by the landlord. Where a good farmhouse was two centuries old, it was nearly always a former manor-house, once belonging to some family of small squires. (Clapham II, p. 505–512.)

The English landlord, if not a philanthropist, was not a mere 'business man' dealing with land for profit. The rent of the new 'estate cottages' seldom covered the expense of their building and maintenance. There were of course bad landlords, and as a rule the squire had insufficient sympathy with the labourers' desire for a better standard of life, as was shown during the attempt of Joseph Arch to secure them higher wages, by forming agricultural unions (1872–1873). But the English rural landlord did much for the countryside and its inhabitants, whereas the rural landlord of Ireland, like the town landlord of England, was a mere exploiter of other people's labour. The ill odour into which the town landlord most justly fell, made the radical and socialist of the town regard all 'landlords' with too indiscriminate reprobation, and helped to increase his misunderstanding of rural questions.

Thus, when British agriculture reached its peak of prosperity about 1870, prior to the sudden catastrophe of the next decade, it was based on an aristocratic social system, the 'dual ownership' of landlord and farmer, which had done marvels in the way of production, but gave too little of the increased dividend of rural life to the field labourer. It is true that he received higher wages than agricultural labourers on the Continent, but by English standards they were not high. It is true he was materially better off than most of the self-employed peasantry of Europe. It is true also that there were in England many small-sized farms run on a family basis. But there was no longer an independent peasantry as numerous in proportion to the other inhabitants of the country as had once existed in England and still exists in continental countries. The consequence was that when after 1875 Free Trade completed its work by destroying the prosperity of British agriculture, the town-bred electorate was indifferent to

§85
The opening of the
Stockton and Darlington
Railway (1825)

§86 Railway excavation, Camden Town (1839)

§87 Locomotive sheds, Camden Town (1839)

§88 Pangbourne Station (1846)

§89 Bristol Station (1846).
(*Note the ecclesiastical 'gothic' of the architecture*)

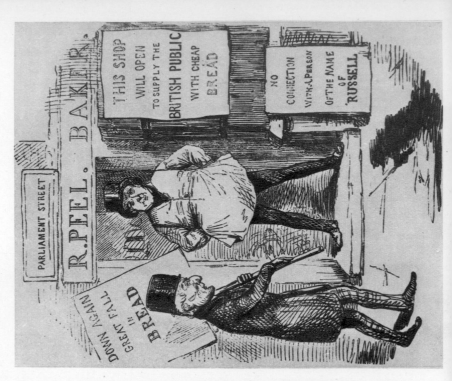

§92 "Emigration a Remedy" (1848)

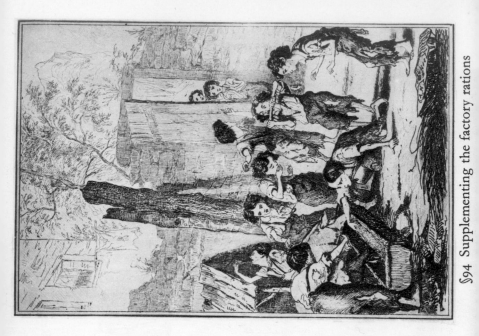

§93 Inside a mill

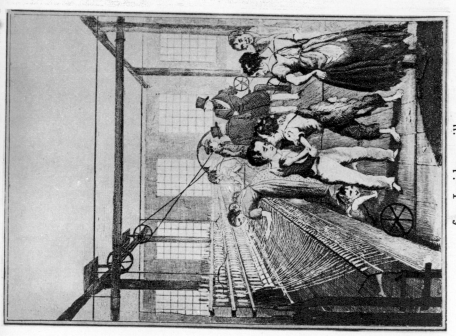

§94 Supplementing the factory rations

§95 Anti-Slavery Convention (1840)

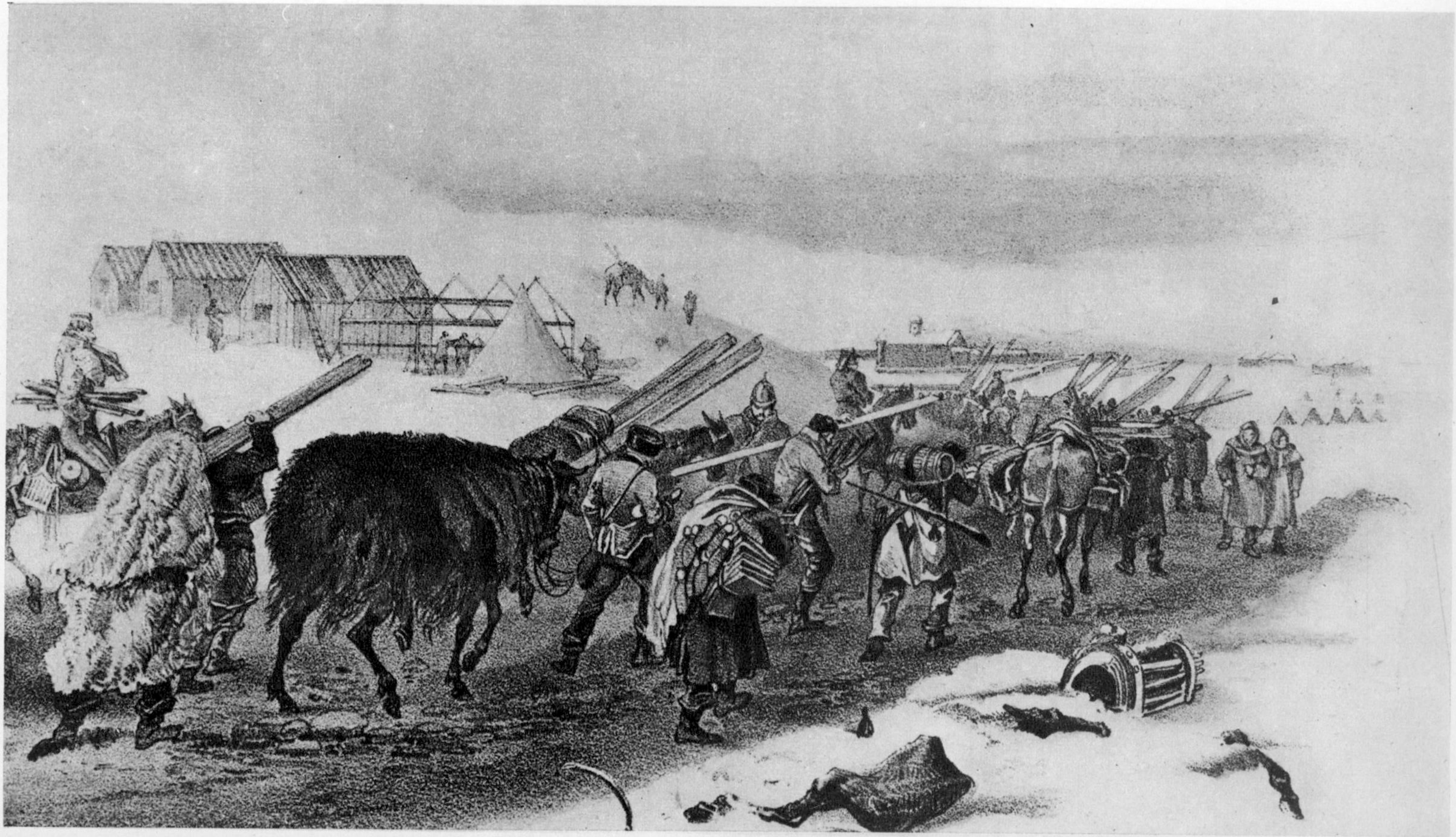

§97 Florence Nightingale in the hospital at Scutari

§98 Alfred Tennyson

§99 William Morris

100 W. E. Gladstone

§101 Charles Darwin

§102 A dinner party in 1882

§103 Late for Dinner (1886)

*Mary Jane:* "They've all sat down some time, Sir!"

*Effie:* "Oh! Never mind! You come on the stairs with us, and have the things as they come out."

§104 Conversation piece in 1866

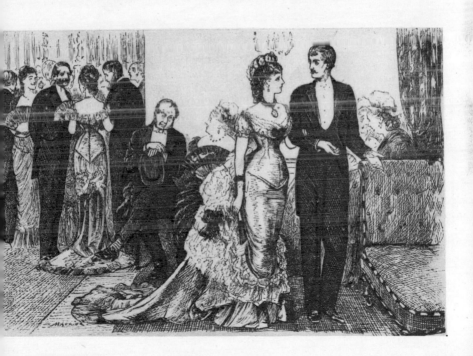

§105 A ball-dress in 1878

"I should like to sit down but my dressmaker says I mustn't."

§106 A formal interior in 1878.  The Music Room

§107 "A cup of tea and a quiet cigarette after lunch"

§108 "Women were becoming more athletic" (1883)

§109 A picnic in 1887

§110 A sportswoman of 1885

§111 Clubwomen of 1878

The emancipation of women.

the decay of rural life—because it was associated with an aristocratic system. Too many Englishmen looked on almost with
satisfaction at the progress of the national disaster, as being a free
and natural economic change.

The passing of the Reform Bill of 1832 was at once followed
in the industrial North by a fierce agitation of the factory hands
against the hard conditions of their lives, particularly in the
matter of hours. In Yorkshire it was to some extent a Radical
and Tory coalition. At Westminster members of all parties took
part in it, and in 1833 the Whig government gave it legislative
form. The principal leaders in the country, Oastler, Sadler and
Shaftesbury, were Tories; they were also all three Evangelicals.
Evangelical humanity was a strong motive in providing the
educated leaders, while the popular drive behind the movement
came from the factory population itself, who were mostly
Radicals. But the Tory country gentlemen were not hostile to
the movement, for they were jealous of the parvenus of the master-
manufacturer class. The squires were incensed at the attacks
made by these upstarts upon the gentlemen of England for
grinding the faces of the poor with their corn-laws; they replied
by denouncing the evils of factory employment, though their
fathers had scouted all such Luddite complaints as 'Jacobinical.'
The split in the ranks of the well-to-do gave the wage earner a
hole through which to thrust his head, and make his case heard.
And behind these class recriminations lay the genuine humanitarianism of the age, focused by the Evangelicals, but not
confined to any religious sect or political party.

The sentiment of humanity was now a great force in politics.
In 1833 it abolished slavery in the Empire at a cost of twenty
million pounds cheerfully paid by the British taxpayer. That
same year it stopped the abuse of children's labour in the textile
factories at home. [See § 93, 94, 95.]

The promoters of Factory legislation found that the appeal
to humanity was most easily made about the children.

It is true [writes Mons. Halévy] that the operatives were seeking a
restriction of working hours for themselves—not for the children who
were very often the victims of their brutality rather than of the employer's tyranny. But the number of children employed in the factories
was so great in proportion to the adults that it was out of the question

6                              81

to restrict the working hours of children without restricting at the same time the hours of the adults. It was for the children that Oastler sought to awaken the pity of the English middle class, but his aim was the legal protection of the adult worker. (Halévy's *Hist. Eng. People*, transl. by Watkin, III, p. 111.)

Lord Althorp's Factory Act of 1833 set legal limits to the working hours of children and young persons respectively, and its provisions were enforced by the appointment of factory inspectors, with power of entry into the factories. Their appointment had been suggested by some of the better disposed among the employers themselves. For it was not merely bad employers but bad parents living on their children's labours, who required watching. Moreover, the better employers wanted the government to prevent the worse employers from undercutting them by defying this Act as they had defied the earlier laws.

Out of this children's charter of 1833 grew the Ten Hours Bill. This second crisis of Factory legislation came to a head in 1844–1847, contemporaneously with the repeal of the Corn Laws, and was heated with the fires of that great dispute. The Ten Hours Bill limited the daily work of women and youths in textile factories, and thereby compelled the stoppage of all work after ten hours, as the grown men could not carry on the processes alone. This measure had for years been the aspiration of the employees and the storm-centre of a fierce controversy. In Parliament it produced curious cross-voting. Among the Liberals— Melbourne, Cobden and Bright were against it: Russell, Palmerston and Macaulay were for it. And the Conservatives were no less divided, Peel being strongly against the Bill, while a majority of the Protectionist squires voted in its favour. But the man who finally carried the Bill through the House of Commons was Fielden, 'the largest cotton spinner in England; and the man who told with him in the lobby had passed from the position of worker to that of employer in the same industry.' (Hammond, *Lord Shaftesbury*, p. 121 and *passim*.)

What the Reform Bill of 1832 was to all later extensions of the Franchise, the Factory Acts of 1833 and 1847 are to the far-spreading code of statutory regulation which now governs the conditions and hours of almost all branches of industry. The factory system which at its first coming bade fair to destroy the health and happiness of the race, has been gradually converted into an instrument to level up the average material conditions under which labour is carried on. It is far easier to inspect factories than it would ever have been to inspect the old system of domestic work. Robert Owen's vision of decent conditions of life for factory hands, which he had first embodied in his own New Lanark Mills, was destined in the course of a hundred years to be made the standard for the greater part of the industrial world. And the decisive first steps were taken in 1833 and 1847, during the period which it is usual to condemn as obsessed by the doctrine of *laissez-faire*. It is difficult to obsess people with a doctrine if once either their hearts or their pockets are touched. A former generation, in anti-Jacobin days, being in a mood to grind the faces of the poor, had chosen out those parts of *laissez-faire* which suited their purpose and neglected the rest. Now the process was being reversed: the self-same House of Commons that repealed the Corn Laws in the name of *laissez-faire* passed the Ten Hours Bill in flat defiance of that doctrine. At no period was *laissez-faire* in force in all directions at once. Benthamism was in many respects its exact opposite, calling for the creation of organs of government to control and harmonize the rival interests of society.

In the years following the Ten Hours Bill of 1847, the principle of factory regulation was extended by a series of Acts to other manufactures besides textiles. And the revelation of the appalling conditions of female and child labour in the coal-mines, an evil several centuries old, had led to Lord Shaftesbury's Mines Act of 1842, by which the underground employment of women and of children under ten was forbidden. By an Act of 1850 adult males were also protected by a Mines Inspectorate, and step by step the provision of safety in the Mines became the care of the State.

The gross ill-usage of little boys as sweeps, by masters who found it cheaper to drive them through the soot-choked chimneys than to use a long brush, had been exposed to the public indignation, but in vain. In 1875 Shaftesbury wrote in his diary: 'One hundred and two years have elapsed since the good Jonas Hanway brought the brutal iniquity before the public, yet in many parts of England and Ireland it still prevails with the full knowledge and consent of thousands of all classes.' That year Shaftesbury obtained the passing of an Act that at last cured the evil. The previous Acts of 1840 and 1864 had been rendered dead letters by the callous connivance of private householders, local authorities and magistrates. (Hammond, *Lord Shaftesbury*, chap. XV.)

The passing of the abortive chimney-sweeper's Act of 1864 had been in large measure due to the publication in the previous years of Charles Kingsley's *Water Babies*, describing the relations of little Tom to his master Grimes. Dickens had already done much to interest the public in the sufferings and feelings of children; *Water Babies* did that and it did something more, it created a fairy world of fantasy and fun which grown-ups and children could share together. The sympathetic interest in the games, fancies and thoughts of children was one of the best features of an age that thought much of family life, and reared numerous offspring. In the middle years of the Century, Grimm's and Andersen's fairy tales came over from the Continent and conquered England. Boys' and girls' story books were multiplied apace. Children's books of which the pleasure was intended to be shared with grown-ups was a characteristic invention of the time. In the previous century *Gulliver* and *Robinson Crusoe* had been written for men and women, though children and boys delighted in them and in the *Arabian Nights*. But in 1855 Thackeray published the *Rose and the Ring, a Fireside Pantomime for great and small children*, and ten years later *Alice*, written for the little daughter of the Dean of Christ Church, was published by 'Lewis Carroll.' These masterpieces of a peculiar type of literature have since been imitated by a host of writers, including Stevenson, Barrie and Andrew Lang.

This enlarged sympathy with children was one of the chief contributions made by the Victorian English to real civilization. But such feelings were not universal, as the long delay over the chimney-sweep scandal testified. Neglect and ill-usage of children died hard. The streets of the slums were still the only playground for the majority of city children, few of whom had schools to go to until 1870, and none of whom had Play Centres till the turn of the Century. The Society for the Prevention of Cruelty to Children was not founded till 1884; since that year it has dealt effectively with more than five million cases. The Nineteenth Century saw the gradual disuse of cruel flogging of boys, which educational reformers had deplored in vain for ages past. In many directions life was being humanized, as some set-off against its increasing ugliness and sordidness in the growth of great cities under their pall of soot and fog.

Disraeli's famous saying that England was divided into two nations, the rich and the poor, had in it an uncomfortable amount of truth. But like all epigrams it was only half true. Certainly the Industrial Revolution had in the Victorian era increased the disparity of wealth between the very rich and the very poor, and had segregated classes geographically by substituting great cities divided into various social quarters, in place of the life of villages and market towns with some features and interests common to all. But industrial change had also increased the number of middle classes of varying levels of wealth and comfort; and it had raised the standard of life of the better-to-do working classes, such as engineers, far above that of the unskilled labourer and slum-dweller. There were many more 'nations' than two; if only two were to be reckoned, it would have taxed the wit of Disraeli himself to say where the line was to be drawn. [See § 82, 83.]

The improvement of the lot of the wage-earners in the 'fifties and 'sixties, was partly due to the prosperity of trade in those fortunate years when England was the workshop of the world; partly to the social legislation of Parliament; and partly to Trade Union action to raise wages, and stop truck payments and other abuses. Trade Unionism was particularly strong among the working-class aristocracy, the engineers and the men of other skilled trades.

To this period also belongs the growth of the Co-operative movement, which has done so much to stop the exploitation of the consumer by the retail dealer, and to train the working classes in self-government and business management. It originated from the enterprise of two dozen Chartist and Owenite workmen of Rochdale, who in 1844 opened in Toad ('T'owd) Lane the store of the Rochdale Pioneers. It was a humble affair, and many larger attempts at co-operation had failed. But these men chanced to have hit on the right plan for realizing Owen's dream. Their rules were—the sale of goods at market prices, followed by division of surplus profit among members in proportion to their purchases. This secured democratic interest in the management of the business, while eliminating profit at the expense of the

consumer. It was on these lines that the Co-operative movement
reached such enormous development before the century closed.

The practical success of the movement was helped in the
'fifties by the zeal with which its idealist aspect was preached both
by the Secularists led by Holyoake, the pupil of Owen, and by
the Christian Socialists whom Frederick Denison Maurice had
inspired, especially Tom Hughes, the author of *Tom Brown's
Schooldays*. The attempts of the shopkeepers to establish a boy-
cott of the movement only increased its strength. In the 'seventies
the Co-operative Societies added production on a considerable
scale to their original activities.

The Co-operative movement was of more than financial importance. It gave many working people a sense that they also
had 'a stake in the country.' It taught them business habits and
mutual self-help, and drew them together in societies that
encouraged the desire for education and self-improvement. 'It
is,' writes one of its historians, 'in its intellectual and moral
influence upon its members, even more than the financial savings
that it effects and encourages, that the Co-operative movement
has wrought a beneficent revolution among tens of thousands of
working-class families, and has contributed so largely to the social
transformation of Great Britain.'

The expedients by which the new Britain was striving to
remedy the evils attendant on the Industrial Revolution—
Co-operation, Factory Laws, Trade Unionism, Free Trade—
were all, like the Industrial Revolution itself, British in conception
and origin.

The second quarter of the Nineteenth Century was the period
in the settlement of Canada, Australia and New Zealand, which
decided that those lands should be peopled mainly from Britain
and should become parts of a free British Commonwealth of
Nations.

The overpeopling of Great Britain deplored by Malthus, and
the sorry plight of the English peasantry at home, caused in
these years the great rural exodus to the Colonies on which the
modern Empire was rebuilt. [See § 92.] The tide of emigration
also ran strongly to the United States, and might have run there
almost to the exclusion of British territories but for the organized
effort of emigration societies, and the occasional assistance of

Government, inspired by the propaganda of Gibbon Wakefield. He preached to his countrymen that emigration was the true relief of their economic miseries, and that the colonies need not

The Navvy. ('Terrible conditions in the Army in the Crimea being greatly increased for want of roads a corps of navvies was sent out' (1855))

in all cases be mere ports of call or places of trade, but might become new British nations. To him is largely due the systematized and aided emigration that founded modern Canada, Australia and New Zealand.

The condition of England's happiness in the Nineteenth Century, and the cause of that peculiar belief in ' progress ' as a law of history which cheered the Victorian mind, was the fact that we were not engaged in any great war for a hundred years after Waterloo. The Crimean War (1854–1856) was no exception. It was merely a foolish expedition to the Black Sea, made for no sufficient reason, because the English people were bored by peace, in spite of the flood of pacifist talk in which they had been indulged three years before at the time of the Great Exhibition in Hyde Park. The bourgeois democracy, played upon by its favourite newspapers, was worked up to crusading ardour on behalf of Turkish rule over the Balkan Christians, which in the following generation the same forces, when led by Gladstone, precisely reversed. We fought the Crimean War on a principle of limited liability and broke it off when the desire for foreign adventure had been satisfied. It is a fact in our social history that foreign policy was becoming less of a mystery of statesmen and more of an interest of the people at large. Whether statesmen or people have been most foolish it is perhaps difficult to say.

But the Crimean War had one serious and beneficent consequence, the institution of nursing as a profession for trained women of a better type than Mrs. Gamp. The astonishing personal success of Florence Nightingale lay in the forcing of her modern methods of hospital management on the Crimean Army authorities, who in all else were so antiquated: they would not even make a railway for the few miles from Balaclava port to the siege lines before Sebastopol, till compelled by the public opinion at home, stirred up by the press and its first 'War Correspondents.' [See § 96, 97.]

The idea of nursing as a serious profession, thus advertised by the sensations of the Crimean War, spread fast in civil life and soon made a new era in public health and medical practice. Moreover, the idea of training women to professions, due to Florence Nightingale's initiative, invaded other spheres of life besides nursing. The ideals of the age of Scott and Byron had demanded that a lady should prove her ladyhood bv the beauty of idleness and by touching dependence upon her male protectors. But in the last half of Victoria's reign a very different idea began to gain ground, namely that upper and middle class women, more particularly the unmarried, should be trained to support themselves and to be of some use to the world.

The Crimean War had also its effects in lesser matters. In imitation of our heroes in the trenches before Sebastopol, smoking became fashionable again after being banished from polite circles for eighty years. For the same reason beards returned after an absence from well-bred society of two centuries. The typical mid-Victorian of all classes was a man with a beard and a pipe.

It was the era of 'muscular Christianity,' strenuousness and cold baths. Organized games, particularly cricket and football, were spreading fast in schools, Universities and in ordinary life. Walking and the new diversion of mountain climbing were characteristic of an energetic and athletic generation; even ladies were now allowed to walk. The days of lawn tennis had not yet come, and could scarcely have come so long as the hampering crinoline was in fashion. But ladies and gentlemen contended in the milder tournaments of the croquet lawn, where sometimes a member of the fair sex, in preparing her stroke, would gently move the ball into a more favourable position under the ample cover of the crinoline!

One thing that the Crimean War did not produce was Army Reform. It was indeed recognized that though the veteran soldiers had fought well, maintaining the regimental traditions inherited from the Peninsula, they had been ill supplied with recruits, ill fed and ill organized as an army. But the army recovered its prestige next year in the Indian Mutiny, when the Victorian virtues of self-help and individual initiative showed at their best. [See § 84.] And in any case the reformers of that age were not interested in the army. They regarded it as a hopelessly aristocratic institution, not really needed by a civilized State. They were concerned not to gain security by improving it, but to save money by cutting it down.

Only in 1859 there was a panic over the supposed ill intentions of Napoleon III, though his real desire was to live on friendly terms with England. So the islanders had one of their periodic frights that punctuated their perpetual unpreparedness, and the result on this occasion was the starting of the Volunteer movement, the drilling of business men and their employees in off hours, consonant with the civilian and individualist spirit of the time. But the reform of the regular army remained unattempted, until the Franco-Prussian war of 1870 made the English public vaguely aware that something was going on among those unaccountable foreigners. And on this occasion panic fortunately produced the Cardwell reforms, which included the abolition of the purchase of officers' commissions, and the short service system of enlistment, creating at last an army reserve.

*Chapter Four*

# THE SECOND HALF OF THE VICTORIAN ERA,
## 1865–1901

ONE of the difficulties of an attempt to write the social as distinct from the political history of a nation is the absence of determining events and positive dates by which the course of things can be charted. The social customs of men and women and their economic circumstances, particularly in modern times, are always in movement, but they never change completely or all at once. The old overlaps the new so much that it is often a question whether to ascribe some tendency in thought or practice to one generation or the next.

But on the whole the most marked changes of tendency in Victorian England may be ascribed to the later 'sixties and the 'seventies. The old landmarks are still there, but they are no longer so prominent. The territorial aristocracy still rules the rural parts, and still leads society in London and in its country-house gatherings; the individualist business man still flourishes, with the honest, limited virtues of bourgeois self-help. But these classes no longer fill so much of the scene as in the days of Palmerston and Peel; and the ideas or lack of ideas for which they stand are challenged now by others beside 'low Radicals.' In all ranks of life free debate of social customs and religious beliefs is taking the place of the settled creeds of the early Victorian era. John Stuart Mill in his *Liberty* (1859) preached the doctrine of revolt against the tame acceptance of conventional opinions, and a dozen years later, such an attitude has become very general. It is a liberal, outspoken age, whose most representative men are neither the aristocrats nor the shopkeepers, but men of University education, or of trained professional intelligence, readers of Mill, Darwin, Huxley and Matthew Arnold, George Eliot and Browning—the gentlemanly bearded intellectuals whose family life Du Maurier delighted to delineate in the pages of *Punch*. [See § 125.]

Democracy, bureaucracy, collectivism are all advancing like a silent tide making in by a hundred creeks and inlets. A short list of some of the changes which marked off the 'seventies from the previous generation, may at least be suggestive. The impact of Darwinism on the Bible religion of the English was being widely, though not yet universally, felt; in 1871 Oxford and Cambridge were thrown open to all irrespective of religious belief; science and history were rapidly taking their place beside classics and mathematics in the academic world; in 1870 competitive examination was made the normal method of entry to the Civil Service, in order to enlist the ablest young men from the Universities in the new bureaucracy; the working men of the towns had received the Parliamentary franchise by the Reform Bill of 1867; and three years later Forster's Act provided primary education for all; by the legislation of 1871–1875 the Trade Unions received a new Charter of rights corresponding to their growing power; in business administration, limited liability companies were taking the place of the old family firms; the professional and social emancipation of women went forward on the lines advocated in Mill's *Subjection of Women* (1869); women's colleges were founded at Oxford and Cambridge and women's secondary schools were much improved; the Married Women's Property Act released the wife, if she had money of her own, from economic bondage to her husband: the 'equality of the sexes' began to be advocated in theory, and found its way increasingly into the practice of all classes. The demand for the political enfranchisement of women was the outcome of a very considerable degree of social enfranchisement already accomplished.

But the greatest single event of the 'seventies, fraught with immeasurable consequences for the future, was the sudden collapse of English agriculture.

From 1875 onwards the catastrophe set in. A series of bad seasons aggravated its initial stages, but the cause was the development of the American prairies as grain lands within reach of the English market. The new agricultural machinery enabled the farmers of the Middle-West to skim the cream off virgin soils of unlimited expanse; the new railway system carried the produce to the ports; the new steamers bore it across the Atlantic. English agriculture was more scientific and more highly capitalized than American, but under these conditions the odds were too great.

Mass production of crops by a simpler and cheaper process undercut the elaborate and expensive methods of farming which had been built up on well-managed English estates during the previous two hundred years. The overthrow of the British landed aristocracy by the far-distant democracy of American farmers was one outcome of this change of economic circumstance. An even more important consequence has been the general divorce of Englishmen from life in contact with nature, which in all previous ages had helped to form the mind and the imagination of the island race.

The other States of Europe, which still had peasantry and valued them as a stabilizing element in the social fabric, warded off the influx of American food by tariffs. But in England no such policy was adopted or even seriously considered. The belief in Free Trade as the secret of our vast prosperity, the unwillingness to interfere with the world-commerce on which our power and wealth seemed to stand secure, the predominance of the towns over the country in numbers and still more in intellectual and political leadership, the memories of the 'hungry 'forties' when the Corn Laws had made bread dear for the poor—all these circumstances prevented any effort to save the rural way of life. Least of all did the late Victorians see any need to grow food in the island to provide for the necessities of future wars. After two generations of the safety won at Waterloo, real national danger seemed to have passed away for ever, like a dream of

> Old unhappy far-off things
> And battles long ago.

In 1846 Disraeli had prophesied the ruin of agriculture as an inevitable result of Free Trade in corn. For thirty years he had been wrong. Now he was suddenly right—and now he was Prime Minister. Yet he did nothing about it, and allowed the 'curse of Cobden' to blight the English cornfields. Immersed in oriental policies, the old man made no attempt to oppose the spirit of the age at home, to which in fact he had become a convert.

Statesmen regarded the fate of agriculture with all the more indifference because it involved no acute problem of unemployment. The farm labourer did not remain on the land when his occupation there was gone, as unemployed miners hang round a closed mine. When 'Hodge' lost his job, or when his wages fell, he slipped away to the towns and found work there. Or else he migrated overseas, for the Colonies and the United States were still receiving the overplus of our still rapidly rising population. As a class, the English agricultural labourer was well accustomed to the idea of leaving the land. He could not love the fields that he tilled as a hireling for others, as passionately as the Irish peasant loved the plot of earth from which he wrung the food of his family and which he regarded as by right his own. The English rustic moreover, knew more about the town and the opportunities and the wages it offered. He had the desire characteristic of our people to 'better himself,' and so he raised no outcry when this involved exile from the scenes of his boyhood.

Meanwhile the landlords and farmers, who had neither the wish nor the power to divorce themselves from the soil, suffered and complained in vain, for their day as the political rulers of England had gone by. Both the Liberal and the Conservative intelligentsia of the 'seventies and eighties were saturated with the Free Trade Doctrine: they believed that if one industry, agriculture for instance, went under in free competition, other industries would gain proportionately and would take its place—and so all would be well. But all was not well. For political economy does not cover the whole field of human welfare. The men of theory failed to perceive that agriculture is not merely one industry among many, but is a way of life, unique and irreplaceable in its human and spiritual values.

In the first decade of the decline that began in 1875, the acreage of wheat in England fell by nearly a million acres. Already in 1881 there were some hundred thousand fewer farm-labourers than ten years before, and that was only the beginning of the exodus. Whole regions of cornland in the West, Midlands and North were laid down in grass, but without any corresponding rise in the number of livestock, though there was a considerable substitution of cattle for sheep. The introduction of frozen meat from Australia, New Zealand and South America was a new feature of the 'eighties and 'nineties. From 1891-1899 a second wave of agricultural depression followed, as severe as that of 1875–1884. By the end of the Century the corn area in England and Wales had shrunk from over eight million acres in 1871 to under six million. Permanent pasture had greatly increased, but the fall in cattle and sheep prices kept pace with the fall in the price of corn. And the agricultural labourers, in spite of the fact that they had been given the franchise in 1884, continued to flock into the towns or to pass oversea.

The historian of English farming thus epitomizes the last decades of Victoria's reign:

> The legislature was powerless to provide any substantial help. Food was, so to speak, the currency in which foreign nations paid for English manufactured goods, and its cheapness was an undoubted blessing to the wage-earning community. Thrown on their own resources, agriculturalists fought the unequal contest with courage and tenacity. But as time went on, the stress told more and more heavily. Manufacturing populations seemed to seek food-markets everywhere except at home. Enterprise gradually weakened; landlords lost their ability to help, farmers their recuperative power. Prolonged depression checked costly improvements. Drainage was practically discontinued. Both owners and occupiers were engaged in the task of making both ends meet on vanishing incomes. Land deteriorated in condition; less labour was employed; less stock was kept; bills for cake and fertilizers were reduced. The counties which suffered most were the corn-growing districts, in which high farming had won its most signal triumphs. (Ernle, *English Farming*, p. 379.)

The damage indeed was the greater because English agriculture was a highly capitalized system for producing the staple products —corn, particularly wheat so costly to grow in most parts of England, and the best sheep and cattle in the world. Other uses of land had been unduly neglected. There was a fixed acreage of hops, chiefly in Kent. But potatoes occupied only two per cent. of the cultivated area. Not enough had been done either with fruit or vegetables. Market gardening had never been systematically organized.

Neither the small cultivators nor the State were playing their proper part. It was only after the war of 1914–1918 that the State undertook the large-scale forestry which it is specially fitted to conduct. The landlords, who had planted diligently in the Eighteenth and early Nineteenth Centuries, lost interest in forestry as a trade, when government no longer required great oaks to build our battleships, and when timber of all other sorts poured in from Scandinavia and North America at prices that discouraged the home-grower. The vast demand for pit-props and for builder's wood was supplied from oversea.

England in 1880 could boast of finer trees than any other country, if judged by aesthetic, not by commercial standards. The forests had all gone, save a patch or two like the New Forest and the Forest of Dean. Yet seen from the air, the landscape would not have appeared ill wooded. The trees were hedgerow timber scattered over the countryside, or park trees preserved for their beauty, or coverts planted for game. Estate agents were not interested in timber values and neglected to remove ivy, to thin out, and to cut and sell at the right time. The conifer was creeping in for the purpose of the new plantations, and so was the rhododendron, approved by the taste of that age. Both were exotic in most parts of the island, but both were well fitted to lodge the 'kept cock pheasant, master of many a shire,' whom the youthful Kipling disliked as the symbol of an England going to fat, in a dream of wealth and peace that might some day have a rude awakening.

The fate of agriculture was only one example of the near-sightedness characteristic of English State policy. The later Victorians laid no far plans for the future. They were content to meet those demands and to solve those problems of which the pressure was already felt. But within those limits they were more active reformers than their self-satisfied fathers of the Palmerstonian era: they brought up to date the civil service, local government, education, Universities—and even to a limited extent the army.

For the English had already lost some of the complacency and cocksureness of the 'fifties and 'sixties. In those lucky days gone by, England had manufactured for a world that was still a generation behind her in industrial machinery; there had been no military power more formidable or more hostile than the France of Napoleon III; in 1848, the year of Continental Revolution and Reaction, Macaulay's countrymen had rejoiced to think that in wealth, in liberty and in order our country was ahead of every other, 'the envy of less happier lands.' The Franco-Prussian war of 1870 was the first shock. And during the three following decades America and Germany rose as manufacturing powers rival to our own. The immensely greater natural resources of America, the scientific and technical education provided by far-sighted governments in Germany, told more and more every year. To meet this new situation, our island liberty, Free Trade and individualist self-help might not alone be enough. Some sense of this led to improved technical education over here. It led, also, to greater interest in our own 'lands beyond the sea,' the Imperialist movement of the 'nineties; and it induced a more friendly and respectful attitude to America than our political classes had shown during her Civil War at the end of the Palmerstonian epoch. The democratic England of the new era was better able to understand both the United States and 'the Colonies,' as Canada and Australasia were still called.

The new situation led also to an anxious interest in modern Germany, which our countrymen until 1870 had been content to ignore. In that fateful year two books, Matthew Arnold's *Friendship's Garland* and George Meredith's *Harry Richmond* warned England that national education and national discipline in the Teutonic heart of Europe was creating a new kind of power that had a jealous eye on our easily won, carelessly guarded, ill-distributed wealth. At the same time Ruskin nobly spent the popularity and influence which he had won as interpreter of art and nature, in a new role as social prophet, denouncing the ill employment of our boasted wealth in destroying beauty, and its ill distribution so corrupting alike to the superfluously rich and the miserably poor.

There was no strong movement of socialism among the working class till the last years of the Century, but discontent with the spirit of *laissez-faire* had been growing long before. John Stuart Mill died in 1873, bequeathing a testament of neo-liberal philosophy that strongly influenced the thought and practice of the age that followed. Mill's doctrine was semi-socialistic. He urged the better distribution of wealth by direct taxation, particularly taxes on inheritance; the bettering of conditions of life by social legislation enforced by an effective bureaucracy, national and local; a complete system of manhood and womanhood suffrage not only for Parliament but for the bodies entrusted with local government. In Mill's thought, democracy and bureaucracy were to work together, and it is largely on these lines that the social fabric of modern England has in fact been constructed, even after Mill himself and his philosophy had passed out of fashion.

§112 A London fog (1876)

§113 Ramsgate sands in 1861

§114 Pegwell Bay in 1858
"Children and their parents bathed and dug and searched the
tidal treasures of the rocks"

§115 A seaside resort in the 90's

On the Spa, Scarborough.

§116 August at Scarborough (1899)

§117 Riders and strollers in the Park (1885)

§118 The Eton and Harrow match at Lords (1878)

§119 Sir Gorgius Midas at home (1878)

§120 Aestheticism (1873)

> *Tom:* "I say, old man, now you've got that stunning house of yours, you ought to be looking out for a wife!"
>
> *Rodolphus:* "Quite so. I was thinking of one of those Miss Gibsons, don't you know—"
>
> *Tom:* "Ah! let me recommend the *tall* one, old man. She'll make the best wife in the world!"
>
> *Rodolphus:* "Quite so. But the *short* one seems to harmonise better with the kind of *furniture* I go in for—*buhl* and *marqueterie*, don't you know."

§121 Large families (1878)

§122 Armies of servants (1883)

§123 A young ladies' seminary (1876)

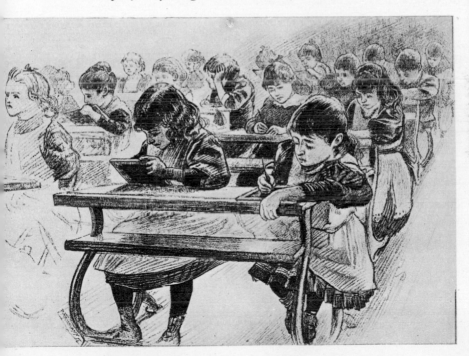

§124 Free Education—Arithmetic (1891)

§125 "The joys of photography" (1886)

§126 Speaking to Paris from London by telephone (1891)

§127 "In the nineties the bicycle became fashionable"—
American tourists in England (1899)

§128 Easter on a motor-car. A steep run to Tunbridge (1898)

§129 A steam bus in 1898

§130 Naval manoeuvres in 1893—"Steam Tactics"

§131 The old Alhambra and advertising in the 90's

§132 The theatre of the *Fin de siècle*

§133 The "city" in 1897

§134 Crowds in a London park at the end of the century

§135 "The end of the Queen's last Journey".
The funeral procession leaving Windsor for Frogmore

But in spite of the decay of England's agriculture, in spite of the diminution of her industrial lead over all other nations, in spite of the increasing sense that all was not well with her social system and the conditions of life in her city populations, nevertheless the last thirty years of Victoria's reign were on the whole years of great prosperity and increasing wealth in which most sections of the community shared. The Queen's Jubilees of 1887 and 1897 were celebrated by all classes with real pride and thankfulness, due in part to a sense of delivery from the conditions endured at the beginning of her reign, for the 'hungry 'forties' were still remembered. Manners were gentler, streets were safer, life was more humane, sanitation was improving fast, working-class housing, though still bad, was less bad than ever before. Conditions of labour had been improved, real wages had risen, hours had shortened. But unemployment, sickness and old age, not yet regularly provided for by the State, still had terrors for the workman.

The Free Trade finance of Peel and Gladstone had lifted the weight of taxation from the poor by reducing indirect taxation to a minimum. Yet the income tax in the 'eighties varied from a bare twopence in the pound to a mere sixpence halfpenny. It is now ten shillings (1941), to say nothing of the surtax.

Free Trade, besides relieving the burdens of the poor, also claimed credit for the enormous increase of our shipping and overseas trade. Even our coastal trade had been thrown open to the ships of all nations, but the foreigner had, in open competition, only secured one half of one per cent. of it. And in the 'eighties this coastal trade, which included so large a proportion of home-consumed coal, was greater in cargo tonnage than the whole of our vast overseas commerce. Yet the oceans of the world were the highways of England. In 1885 a third of the world's sea-going ships were on the British register, including four-fifths of the world's steamships. Masts and sails were on the decline, but the fast ocean-going 'clippers' were British, and in 1885 our tonnage under sail was still as large as it had been in 1850, while our steam tonnage was four millions greater.

The tonnage of the port of London was still sixty per cent. greater than that of the Mersey, though Liverpool, dealing in Lancashire's cotton, exported more British goods than the Capital. The great Thames and Mersey docks were both completed in the 'eighties. The railway system had greatly increased the volume of overseas trade, but had further reduced the number of ports, a process begun in the Eighteenth Century. Whitby,

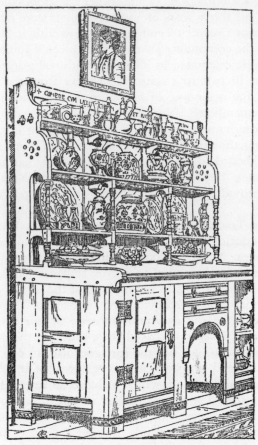

'Reformed' taste in interior decoration (1868).
A dining-room sideboard

Lancaster, Ayr and many other small harbours had now gone the way of Fowey, Chester and the Cinque Ports. But in the last half of the Nineteenth Century, thanks to the railways, Barrow had sprung to greatness out of nothing, and Grimsby out of 'almost nothing.' Southampton had revived, after a long eclipse, for it was now the headquarters of the P. and O. line to the East.

Cardiff had increased its population thirteen-fold, and had just passed Newcastle as the world's greatest coal exporter, though Tyneside, in the great days of Armstrong's Elswick, was itself mightily on the increase. Such was the work of reconstruction of industry and commerce done by the railways. But 'railways had not made Tyneside; it was Tyneside that made them.' (Clapham, II, 519–529.)

Under such conditions of 'free trade' prosperity, many articles that were luxuries in 1837 were common comforts in 1897. Food, clothing, bedding, furniture were far more abundant than in any previous age. [See § 102, 103, 104, 105, 106, 107.] Gas and

Mantelpiece shelves

oil-lighting were giving way to electricity. Holidays by the seaside had become a regular part of life to the lower middle class and even to large sections of the working class, particularly in the North. Already in 1876 Blackpool had grown to the size and status of a Borough, as the scene of the annual holiday of the Lancashire artisan, and he supported Llandudno and the Isle of Man as well. Distant Cornwall was already the holiday resort of the well-to-do at Easter and of the masses in August. In the summer, the lodging-houses in Keswick and Windermere and the farms of the Lake District were thronged with family parties.

Even before the age of railways, Londoners had swarmed on the pier at Brighton and darkened the sands of Margate with their multitude. Now the whole coast of England and Wales was opened out to 'trippers' and 'lodgers,' by steam locomotion and by the increased earnings and savings of all ranks. In remote creeks and fishing hamlets, where families from town came to lodge, children and their parents bathed and dug and searched the tidal treasuries of the rocks; here was at least some mitigation of the divorce of the city-dweller from country life. [See § 113, 114, 115, 116.]

But if seasonal holidays away from home were now common, the 'week-end out of town' was only beginning. It was already a custom among owners of big country houses and their guests, but the 'week-end cottage' for the middle-class family was scarcely yet known. Family church-going and business tradition still kept folk in town for seven days of the week.

Women were becoming more athletic and better walkers as their skirts became somewhat shorter and less redundant [see § 108, 109, 110, 111]; after the disappearance of the crinoline and the long sweeping dress, the active movements of lawn-tennis took the place of croquet in the 'eighties as the game for the encounter of ladies and gentlemen. In the 'nineties the bicycle became fashionable, as soon as the two low wheels succeeded the dangerous 'high bicycle'; this further emancipated women, by sending them out to scour the countryside alone, or in company with the other sex. [See § 127.] The common use of the motor-car and motor-bicycle was still in the future when Victoria died.

While the town-dwellers were learning to explore the by-ways of their own land on foot or on bicycle, others swarmed over France, Switzerland and Italy in greater numbers than ever; they were the chief patrons of the best hotels of Western Europe, of the Mediterranean and of Egypt. And Thomas Cook's 'tours' gave a taste of the delights of continental travel to multitudes of

Iron bedstead with canopy

the thrifty and the humble. In the 'sixties and 'seventies, the period of Leslie Stephen, Whymper and Professor Tyndall, the English, with the help of the splendid race of Swiss guides whom they employed, developed mountain craft on rock and snow, and conquered the great summits of the Alps. In the last decade of the Century rock-climbing in Wales and the Lake District became a skilled pastime at home.

John Buchan in his Memoirs has thus described the London society of his youth, on the eve of the South African War of 1899:

London at the turn of the Century had not yet lost her Georgian air. Her ruling society was aristocratic till Queen Victoria's death and preserved the modes and rites of aristocracy. Her great houses had not disappeared or become blocks of flats. In the summer she was a true city of pleasure, every window box gay with flowers, her streets full of splendid equipages, the Park a show ground for fine horses and handsome men and women. The ritual went far down, for frockcoats and top-hats were the common wear not only for the West End, but about the Law Courts and in the City. On Sunday afternoons we dutifully paid a round of calls. Conversation was not the casual thing it has now become, but was something of an art, in which competence conferred prestige. Also Clubs were still in their hey-dey, their waiting lists were lengthy, membership of the right ones was a stage in a career ... Looking back, that time seems to me unbelievably secure and self-satisfied. The world was friendly and well-bred as I remember it, without the vulgarity and the worship of wealth which appeared with the new century. (*Memory Hold-The-Door*, pp. 92–94.)

Yet already 'society was getting mixed,' and men of mere wealth, like Sir Gorgius Midas in Du Maurier's *Punch* pictures had been prominent in London drawing-rooms for twenty years before the Queen died—the more prominent perhaps for being still somewhat exceptional. [See § 119, 120.] 'Society,' in the older and stricter sense of the term, had still in Palmerston's day been a limited world, its entry closely guarded by certain Whig and Tory Peeresses. But in the 'eighties 'society' had a vaguer meaning, perhaps covering the whole of the upper and professional classes, perhaps including all the well-dressed men and women, who crossed and recrossed each other in Hyde Park parades, or made conversation during the innumerable courses of a London dinner-party. [See § 117, 118.] Yet, as John Buchan truly records, these people maintained, at least in the Capital, a certain aristocratic flavour and convention until the end of the Century. They were different from the well-to-do bourgeois of the provinces, who still in Yorkshire and Lancashire preferred 'high teas' to dress dinners.

In the 'seventies and 'eighties, large families were still customary in the professional and business world, as well as in the working class, and the population rose apace since so many of the children born were now kept alive. The death-rate dropped with the improvement of town sanitation and the constant progress of medical knowledge and practice. In 1866 the excess of births over deaths in England was 13·3, as against Germany's 10·8 and the French 1·4 per thousand.

After 1870, the parents of working-class families had the relief of a universal system of primary education, but even so, it was a hard struggle, and except in school-time the children of the poor still roamed the streets uncared for. In middle-class homes, it was the era of the rocking-horse and Noah's ark: the full nursery and schoolroom were lively, noisy societies, where childish impressions and characters were formed, till Tomkins major, minor and minimus successively went off to the boarding-school, and could no longer be the joy or the plague of their sisters except during the holidays. Governesses, nurses, butlers, housemaids and cooks were still plentiful and their demands for wages and nights out were still moderate. Many of them became attached and valued members of the household; others came and went, dimly recollected. Their services were arduous and essential, for the tall, narrow town-houses of the middle class were not fitted up with labour-saving appliances; armies of maids staggered up the stairs with hot water for the nursery tubs, and coals for every room, that helped to thicken London's fog. [See § 112, 121, 122.]

Only in the 'nineties did it become evident that a reduction was beginning in the size of families, in the first instance in those of the professional and middle classes, charged with heavy 'public-school' fees, and among the better-to-do artisans struggling to keep up a high standard of life. In 1877 a prosecution of Bradlaugh and Mrs. Besant for publishing a neo-Malthusian pamphlet had given methods of birth-control their first national advertisement. But the slum population, of whom these reformers were chiefly thinking, were the slowest to adopt the advice. The families best able to rear children as they should be reared, were, unfortunately, those that became most addicted to 'race suicide' in the coming century.

The 'seventies and 'eighties had been a period not only of large families but of puritanism in ethical and sexual ideas, qualified by the too frequent weakness of human nature in practice. Queen Victoria had put the example of her court on the side of the stricter code. The genuine honesty of most British merchants as men of business had been one of the causes of our great commercial prosperity. The popular heroes of the period—and they were true heroes—were religious men first and foremost: Livingstone the African explorer and missionary; General Gordon the soldier-philanthropist; Lord Shaftesbury and Mr. Gladstone; to these four, so different from one another and from everyone else, life was the service of God. [See § 100.]

But the older and more definite religious beliefs that meant so much to these men were being successfully attacked by the 'Agnostics' of the same period. Yet even the 'Agnostics' were Puritan in feeling and outlook. Matthew Arnold, the prophet of 'culture,' spoke of 'conduct' as 'three parts of life,' though his idea of 'conduct' was neither narrow nor purely negative. The fame and authority enjoyed by George Eliot's novels were largely due to the fact that they were taken by many as 'restating the moral law and process of soul-making, in terms acceptable to the rationalist agnostic conscience.' Carlyle's prophetic utterance in *Sartor* supplied a vague but emphatic creed to many, including Darwin's militant champion Huxley, who defied the clergy at the famous meeting of the British Association in Oxford in the spirit of Luther at Worms. Leslie Stephen's and John Morley's passionate refusal to compromise with dogmas they had come to disbelieve, breathed the unyielding spirit of Seventeenth Century Puritanism. Leslie Stephen had once been a clergyman, and so had J. R. Green, the popular liberal historian. In literature and thought it was a period of quasi-religious movement away from religion.

In its many-sided curiosity and competence, its self-confidence and alertness, this Late Mid-Victorian culture is Greek. In its blend of intellectual adventure and moral conservatism, it is really Athenian. I doubt if any lines of Tennyson were more often quoted by contemporaries than these:

> Let knowledge grow from more to more,
> But more of reverence in us dwell;
> That mind and soul, according well,
> May make one music as before,
> But vaster.

No words could express more perfectly the Victorian ideal of expansion about a central stability. But would anyone guarantee that they are not a translation from Sophocles? (*Daylight and Champaign*, p. 264, G. M. Young.)

The Puritan attitude to life and conduct was inculcated not only by the Bible religion of the mass of the Victorians, but by the Anglo-Catholic religion that had grown out of the Oxford Movement of the 'thirties, and was now spreading wide, with such men as Gladstone and Salisbury among its lay representatives. But Anglo-Catholicism was strongest among the parish clergy, to many of whom it gave a new professional pride and motive, to take the place of the fast vanishing social ascendancy that had once belonged to the 'clergy of the Establishment' as such. The Anglo-Catholic influence made easier some concessions to ordinary human nature, including a less strict observance of the 'Sabbath' than Evangelicals could approve. The gradual modification of the 'English Sunday' has had effects both good and bad. In this transition period, between the overgreat strictness of the past and the entire laxity of the present day, there was much good in the practice of many families who still insisted on 'Sunday reading' of serious though not necessarily religious books. For one day in the week, novels and magazines were laid aside, and great classical literature like the Bible, Pilgrim's Progress and Paradise Lost, besides more secular poetry and history had a chance of perusal which they no longer enjoy.

Not only a modified Sunday observance, but Bible reading and family prayers were common until near the end of the Century. In his study of the effect of Charles Simeon's influence on English life Canon Smyth has written:

Evangelicalism was the religion of the Home; and in this revival of Family worship it won the most signal and the most gracious of its triumphs. It may well be that this revival was virtually restricted to the upper and middle classes of society, especially the latter: but within these limits it was so widely spread that in 1889 the Provost of King's (Cambridge) in a circular letter addressed to the undergraduates of that College on the subject of voluntary attendance at morning Chapel, could write: 'You most of you, come from homes where family prayers are the custom.' . . . Today that pious custom is virtually extinct: not only because the Victorian piety is virtually extinct, but also because the Victorian family is virtually extinct.' (*Simeon and Church Order*, Charles Smyth, 1940, pp. 19–20.)

English religion had been an imposing fabric in the middle of the Nineteenth Century, but there had been a weakness in its foundations which the movement of scientific discovery was certain to undermine: the belief in the verbal inspiration of the Bible was common to the Nonconformists, to the Church Evangelicals and, to a scarcely less degree, to High Churchmen like Bishop Samuel Wilberforce and Mr. Gladstone. Charles Darwin was as unlike Voltaire as any human being could well be; he had no wish to be an iconoclast; he did not regard the Church as 'the infamous'; and in the end she reverently buried him in Westminster Abbey. But his scientific researches led him to conclusions incompatible with the narrative of the early chapters of Genesis which were as much a part of 'the English Bible' as the New Testament itself. More generally speaking, the whole idea of evolution and of 'man descended from a monkey' was totally incompatible with existing religious ideas of creation and of man's central place in the Universe. [See § 101.]

Naturally the religious world took up arms to defend positions of dateless antiquity and prestige. Naturally the younger generation of scientific men rushed to defend their revered chief, and to establish their claim to come to any conclusion to which their researches led, regardless of the cosmogony and chronology of Genesis, and regardless of the ancient traditions of the Church. The strife raged throughout the 'sixties, 'seventies and 'eighties. It came to involve the whole belief in the miraculous, extending into the borders of the New Testament itself. The 'intellectuals' became more and more anti-clerical, anti-religious and materialistic under the stress of the conflict.

During this period of change and strife, causing much personal and family unhappiness and many searchings of heart, the world of educated men and women was rent by a real controversy, which even the English love of compromise could not deny to exist.[1] In the Twentieth Century that storm has rolled away; that battle is ended and its dead are buried. Faith and Denial are both in a different position. The materialism of the scientist of the

[1] People unduly depreciate Tennyson's intellectual acumen, as shown in the poems he wrote in the formative period of his youth before he took to hymning King Arthur's knights. His *In Memoriam,* written in the 'forties, and published in 1850, nine years before the appearance of Darwin's *Origin of Species,* anticipated the poignancy of the struggle between Faith and Science that convulsed the following era. [See § 98.]

'seventies is felt to be as unsatisfactory as the literal truth of all parts of the Bible is felt to be untenable. Both sides wistfully acknowledge that the whole truth about the Universe cannot be discovered in the laboratory or divined by the Church. But where it can be found is a more difficult matter to determine.

The shaking of dogmatic assurance within the pale of the Anglican and Protestant Churches in the latter years of the Nineteenth Century helped the propaganda of the Roman Church, whose undeviating claim to full and certain knowledge appealed to persons who could not bear to be left in doubt. The Irish immigration below, the flow of converts from the fashionable and intellectual classes above, and the high Roman Catholic birth-rate gave to the Roman Communion a very much more important place in English life at the end of Victoria's reign than that which it had enjoyed at the beginning.

In the last half of the Nineteenth Century, Archaeology and History were in rapid progress, and their discoveries strengthened the hands of science in the strife against orthodox beliefs. Lecky's wise *History of Rationalism* (1865) and the over-confident materialism of Buckle's *History of Civilization* (1857) were part of the strong current that carried men away from ancient faiths. An academic 'liberal' party, of great intellectual distinction and very much in earnest, fought the battle to free Oxford and Cambridge from the bondage of Church monopoly, and won it by the Test Act of 1871. The younger Universities of London and Manchester had long enjoyed such freedom as their birthright.[1]

The two older Universities became so far assimilated to the new that before the end of the Queen's reign Oxford and Cambridge were much more lay than clerical in the personnel of their 'dons,' who were, moreover, now allowed to marry while continuing to hold Fellowships. Academic study now embraced physical science and mediaeval and modern history as strongly as the older humanism and mathematics. In the last decades of the Century, Cambridge were represented to the world by great men of science like Clerk Maxwell, Rayleigh and young J. J. Thomson, while Archdeacon Cunningham was founding

---

[1] Most of the Provincial Universities were founded later still, in the first years of the Twentieth Century. The want of a proper system of popular secondary education prior to Balfour's Bill of 1902 was the fundamental reason why the new universities developed so slowly.

Economic History, and the more brilliant genius of Maitland was revealing the common thoughts of mediaeval men through the harsh medium of their law. Even more rapid had been the change at Oxford, which had been dominated, in the early years of the reign, by Newman and his antagonists disputing over the miracles of Saints and the authority of the Fathers. Very different, thirty years later, was the atmosphere of the University, of which the practical and liberal character was represented to the world by Jowett as Master of Balliol, while the scholarship of Stubbs and Gardiner revealed the growth of the English Constitution, and T. H. Green opened out a new scheme of ethical philosophy.

The last half of Victoria's reign was indeed the period when Oxford and Cambridge were most in the public eye. Their reform, particularly the abolition of religious tests for academic posts (1871) was one of the chief political questions of the day. The liberal-minded and highly educated governing class of the 'seventies were more nearly affiliated to the Universities than to the declining aristocracy or the rising plutocracy. Gladstone abolished patronage in all public offices and made competitive examination the normal entrance to the Civil Service. To select men for practical careers on the report of examiners had seemed an absurd proposal to Palmerston and the aristocratic politicians of the previous era. It was a compliment paid to the reputation of the Oxford and Cambridge system of examination for degrees, and it had the effect of making closer than ever the connection of University men with public life. Trained intellect was henceforth to be a young man's best passport, instead of social patronage or fashionable friends. The evils of the Examination system, especially in its effect on school education, were not yet realized, nor were they yet as great as they have since become.

But perhaps the most characteristic achievement of the last years of the reign was the *Dictionary of National Biography*. It was not the undertaking either of a University or of the State. It was initiated and largely financed by a private individual, George Smith the publisher, whose personal friendship with many authors prompted him to this great undertaking. The Dictionary is a monument of the business ability, the enlightened public spirit and the widespread literary and historical scholarship of the Victorian age at its final culmination. It is the best record of a nation's past that any civilization has produced.

It has already been pointed out that the agnosticism of the English revolt against early Victorian religion had no connection with hedonism in theory or in conduct. Only in the 'nineties, the *fin de siècle*, as the time was called, a change in the direction of levity, if not of laxity, was observed, due no doubt in part to the gradual crumbling of definite religious beliefs with which a strict and slightly ascetic moral code had been associated. [See § 131, 132.] When religion had been transformed, from the 'public and documented system of beliefs, practices and aspirations' that it had been when the Queen came to the throne, into a 'provision for personal needs,' it could no longer influence the conduct of those who felt no such need for themselves. The movement away from family prayers and church-going, the movement towards 'week-ends out of town,' towards the race-course and other pleasures, some innocent and some less innocent, was led by the Prince of Wales (afterwards Edward VII) himself, reacting against an unsympathetic mother and an unwise education. This last decade of the Century is the era of the *Yellow Book* and 'art for art's sake.' But its greatest writers, Meredith, Hardy, William Morris [see § 99], Stevenson and Housman, though all opposed to orthodox religion, were each in his own way as deeply 'serious' as the earlier Victorians.

The conflict between science and religion among the educated classes was crudely but effectively reproduced in Charles Bradlaugh's militant atheism, preached on public platforms to mass meetings of working men; while the last great evangelical revival, the Salvation Army, founded by 'General' Booth, brought the enthusiasm of 'conversion,' after Wesley's original fashion, to the army of the homeless and unfed, to the drunkard, the criminal and the harlot. It was significant of the coming era that the Salvation Army was more sensational in its methods than the older Nonconformist bodies. To bring street bands and coloured uniforms into the service of Protestant religion was something new. It was no less significant that the Salvation Army regarded social work and care for the material conditions of the poor and outcast as being an essential part of the Christian mission to the souls of men and women. It was largely for this reason that its power has become a permanent feature in modern English life. It does not depend on revivalism alone.

Another movement, analogous to the Salvation Army in its combination of religious and social motive, was Total Abstinence, or 'Teetotalism.' Drunkenness and excessive expenditure on drink constituted one of the major evils of city life, one of the chief causes of crime and the ruin in families, especially since spirits had largely taken the place of beer. Our great caricaturists had held up the mirror to this unpleasant aspect of English nature, from the days of Hogarth's *Gin Lane* to George Cruikshank's prints of *The Bottle* and *The Drunkard's Children* (1847–1848), which were circulated by tens of thousands. In the years that followed, an organized and largely successful attack was made on the drinking habits of all classes by the 'Blue Ribbon Army': takers of the total abstinence pledge wore the blue ribbon on their breasts, to pledge them in the face of the world to keep their promise. In the 'seventies the Temperance party, specially strong among the Nonconformists[1] became a force in Liberal politics; but there was an element of fanaticism in their legislative proposals to suppress the drink traffic, that long postponed more practical measures. The movement provoked the better led activities of the drink interest; the brewing companies were backed by a great army of shareholders, and in the last decades of the Century they captured the Conservative Party, with whom after 1886 the government of the country principally lay.

Not only 'Teetotalism' but the proper and moderate use of wine and beer were encouraged by the increasing amenity and diminishing monotony of life, by rival amusements and occupations such as reading, music, playing and watching organized games, bicycling and sight-seeing, country and seaside holidays, above all by more active and educated minds and more comfortable homes. All these things helped to counteract the dullard's itch for the bottle in the cupboard, and diminished the attraction of the lights of the 'gin palace' glaring out its promise of warmth and welcome on to the wet inhospitable street. Moreover, the brewing companies were gradually frightened or shamed into a more enlightened policy in the management of the public houses they controlled, making them more decent, more ready to sell other

[1] But all religious bodies promoted the Temperance movement. In 1909 the Church of England Temperance Society contained 639,233 members. Of these 114,444 were pledged to 'total abstinence,' and as many as 486,888 were 'juvenile members.' For it was a regular policy of Temperance Societies to enlist children before they acquired the taste for drink.

things besides drink, less anxious to send their customers away tipsy. And Balfour's Licensing Act of 1904 at length found a practical method of reducing the excessive number of houses of sale.

In the Twentieth Century, drink has found fresh enemies in the cinema at the street corner, and the wireless at home; and the increase of skilled and mechanical employments, particularly the driving of motor-cars, has put a premium on sobriety. Gambling perhaps now does more harm than drink. But when Queen Victoria died, drinking was still a great evil from the top to the bottom of society, more widely prevalent than in our day, but decidedly less than when she came to the throne.

In the Victorian era photography made its effective impact on the world. [See § 125.] Already in 1871 it was acclaimed by an observer as 'the greatest boon that has been conferred on the poorer classes in later years.'

Any one who knows what the worth of family affection is among the lower classes, and who has seen the array of little portraits stuck over a labourer's fireplace, still gathering into one the 'Home' that life is always parting—the boy that has 'gone to Canada,' the 'girl out at service,' the little one with the golden hair that sleeps under the daisies, the old grandfather in the country—will perhaps feel with me that in counteracting the tendencies, social and industrial, which every day are sapping the healthier family affections, the sixpenny photograph is doing more for the poor than all the philanthropists in the world. (*Macmillan's Magazine*, Sept. 1871.)

By the cheapest and most accurate form of portraiture possible, photography had indeed brought to all classes a prolongation of poignant and of delightful memories of the dead, of the absent, of past years, incidents and associations.

Its effect on art was of more doubtful benefit. Many thousands of painters had formerly lived on the demand for portraits of persons, for accurate delineations of events, scenes and buildings and for copies of famous pictures. Photography henceforth supplied all these. By reducing the importance of picture-painting as a trade, and surpassing it in realistic representation of detail, it drove the painter to take refuge more and more in theory, and in a series of intellectualized experiments in Art for Art's sake.

If the English language at the end of Victoria's reign be compared to its predecessor in the last years of Elizabeth, it will be seen that it is the same language: a modern Englishman can easily understand the Bible of 1611, and he can even understand the more idiomatic dialogues of Shakespeare much more easily at any rate than he can understand Chaucer. For the three centuries between Elizabeth and Victoria had been a period of transactions by writing, governed by a literate upper class who defended the language against fundamental changes in grammar or in the structure of existing words. But in another sense the language had changed—from a vehicle of poetry and emotion to a vehicle of science and journalism. An Elizabethan reading a Victorian newspaper article or listening to the conversation of modern educated people, would be bewildered by long words unfamiliar to him which have been formed, usually from the Latin, not for the purposes of poetry like 'the multitudinous seas incarnadine,' but for the prosaic purposes of science and journalism, and for the discussion of social and political problems: *opportunist, minimize, international, centrifugal, commercialism, decentralize, organization,* and the yet more technical terms of physical science—a useful but unlovely jargon.[1]

In the last half of the Nineteenth Century 'capital' and 'labour' were enlarging and perfecting their rival organizations on modern lines. Many an old family firm was replaced by a Limited Liability Company with a bureaucracy of salaried managers. The change met the technological requirements of the new age by engaging a large professional element, and prevented the decline in efficiency that so commonly marred the fortunes of family firms in the second and third generation after the energetic founder. It was, moreover, a step away from individual initiative, towards collectivism and municipal and State-managed business. The Railway Companies, though still private concerns managed for the benefit of shareholders, were very unlike old family businesses. They existed by reason of Acts of Parliament, that conferred on

---

[1] Mr. Pearsall Smith, in his *The English Language* (Home University Library, p. 124) says: 'Science is in many ways the natural enemy of language. Language, either literary or colloquial, demands a rich store of living and vivid words—words which are "thought pictures," and appeal to the senses and also embody our feelings about the objects they describe. But science cares nothing about emotion or vivid presentation; her ideal is a kind of algebraic notation, to be used simply as an instrument of analysis; and for this she rightly prefers dry and abstract terms, taken from some dead language, and deprived of all life and personality.'

them powers and privileges in return for State control. At the same time the great municipalities went into business to supply lighting, trams and other services to the ratepayers.

The growth of the Limited Liability Company and municipal trading had important consequences. Such large, impersonal manipulation of capital and industry greatly increased the numbers and importance of shareholders as a class, an element in the national life representing irresponsible wealth detached from the land and the duties of the landowner; and almost equally detached from the responsible management of business. All through the Nineteenth Century, America, Africa, India, Australasia and parts of Europe, were being developed largely by British capital, and British shareholders were thus being enriched by the world's movement towards industrialization. [See § 126.] Towns like Bournemouth and Eastbourne sprang up to house large 'comfortable' classes who had retired on their incomes, and who had no relation to the rest of the community except that of drawing dividends and occasionally attending a shareholders' meeting to bully the management. On the other hand, 'shareholding' meant leisure and freedom which was used by many of the later Victorians for the highest purposes of a great civilization.

The 'shareholder' as such had no knowledge of the lives, thoughts or needs of the workmen employed by the Company in which he held shares, and his influence on the relations of capital and labour was not good. The paid manager acting for the company was in more direct relation with the men and their demands, but even he had seldom that familiar personal knowledge of the workmen which the employer had often had under the more patriarchal system of the old family business now passing away. Indeed, the mere size of operations and the numbers of workmen involved rendered such personal relations impossible. Fortunately, however, the increasing power and organization of the Trade Unions, at least in all the skilled trades, enabled the workmen to meet on more equal terms the managers of the companies who employed them. The harsh discipline of the strike and lock-out taught the two parties to respect each other's strength and understand the value of fair negotiation.

Under these conditions the increasing national dividend was rather less unevenly distributed between classes. But the distinction between capital and labour, the personal segregation of

8         113

employer from employed in their ordinary lives still went on increasing. The mere fact that philanthropic 'settlements' were formed in working-class districts in order to show the well-meaning bourgeois how the poor lived, was significant of much. Marxian doctrines, therefore, as to the inevitability of the 'class struggle' were rife at the end of the Century; and the more opportunist collectivism preached by the Fabian Society was still more influential.

But these doctrines were too theoretic to affect the English working man very much. It was no theory, but the practical need to defend Trade Union rights against judge-made law that brought Labour into politics to form a party of its own. For the English law courts developed a most unfortunate habit of discovering that liberties which Parliament intended by its Acts to grant to Trade Unions, had not in fact been granted by those Acts at all. By the legislation of 1825, Trade Unions and combinations to raise wages had been legalized—at least so Parliament and everyone else had supposed for forty years. But in 1867, in the Boilermakers' case, the Judges headed by the Lord Chief Justice decided that Unions, being 'in restraint of trade,' were illegal associations. Fortunately, by the Reform Bill of the same year the working classes were granted the Parliamentary franchise and were therefore able to remedy their grievances by constitutional pressure on politicians. Consequently Gladstone's Act of 1871 restored to Unions the right to exist on very favourable terms, and Disraeli's Act of 1875 legalized 'peaceful picketing.'

After that, the Judges left the Trade Unions alone for another generation, during which the movement spread from the skilled to the unskilled trades, particularly in the great strike of the London dockers led by John Burns in 1889. By the end of the Century, Trade Unionism was in most trades and in most regions of England a very powerful weapon of defence for workmen's wages, on the whole wisely used. Then, in 1901, the Judges struck again with their Taff Vale decision, when the work of former Parliaments was again undone, and strike action by Unions was again pronounced illegal. This decision provoked the effective formation of a separate Labour Party in Parliament at the opening of the new Century, and the Act of 1906 which secured to the Trade Unions highly privileged immunity from legal action. But these events belong to another chapter of social history, beyond the date and outside the atmosphere of Victorian England.

The close of the reign and the end of the Century saw the so-called 'feudal' society of the countryside still in being, but under changing conditions indicative of the advance of democracy even in rural England, and the penetration of village life by forces and ideas from the cities. In the following generation, with the coming of motor transport, the intrusion of urban life upon the rural parts became a flood, turning all England into a suburb. But when Victoria died (1901) the process had not gone so far; country roads and lanes were still country roads and lanes, with all their sleepy charm come down from countless centuries, which the invading bicyclist could enjoy without destroying. The 'country houses,' great and small, still flourished, with their shooting parties and their week-end guests from town; and the estate system was still the method by which English agriculture was organized.

But the country houses and the country estates were less than ever supported by agricultural rents, which American imports had lowered and brought into arrear. The pleasures of the country house and the business of the estate system were now financed by money which the owner drew from industry or other investments, or from his income as ground landlord of more distant urban areas. He was still a country gentleman, but he paid for himself by being other things as well. For British agriculture as an economic proposition had collapsed.

Under these circumstances, the estate system, 'feudal' as it might be, was fairly popular in the countryside, because it brought money from the industrial world to support decadent agriculture, and because the squire and his family brought into village life educated interests and friendly leadership.

But even before the coming of the motor-car with the advent of the new century, the old village life was being transformed into something half suburban by newspapers, ideas, visitors and new residents from the cities. The contrast between the democratic city and the 'feudal' countryside, which had characterized Trollope's England in the middle of Victoria's reign, was less marked in the last decades of the Century. As the result of the Education Act of 1870 the agricultural labourer of the next generation and his women folk could all read and write.

Unfortunately, this power was not directed to foster in them an intelligent and loving interest in country life. The new education was devised and inspected by city folk, intent on producing not peasants but clerks. Before Victoria died, the *Daily Mail* was being read on the village ale bench and under the thatch of the cottage. The distinctive rural mentality was suffering urbanization, and local traditions were yielding to nation-wide commonplace.

In the realm of politics also, town and country were becoming assimilated. In 1884 the agricultural working man received the Parliamentary vote, which had been denied to him in 1867 when his brother of the town was enfranchised. Protected by the ballot, the agricultural labourer could vote as he wished, regardless of farmer and landlord. Proof of this was given in the General Election of 1885, the first held under the new Franchise Bill. On that occasion the boroughs voted Conservative, but the counties unexpectedly voted Liberal, in defiance of squire and farmer. The control over English country life which the squire had exercised for so many centuries was in fact drawing to an end, as far as Parliamentary elections were concerned. It followed inevitably that the local government of the counties must also be put on an elective basis.

In 1888 therefore the Local Government Act established elected County Councils as the administrative organs of country life, in place of the patriarchal rule of the Justices of the Peace. The Justices of the Peace were preserved in their judicial capacity as magistrates. But their administrative functions were handed over to the elected County Councils, strengthened a few years later by the creation of elective Urban and Rural District Councils. Thus, more than fifty years after the Municipal Reform Act of 1835 had set up democratic local government in the boroughs, the same principle was applied to the rural districts. It was an irony of fate that the farm hand was given the Parliamentary and local franchise only after the destruction of English agricultural life had set in, with American competition and the fall of food prices. The agricultural labourers, if they stayed in the countryside, could now take part in its government, but in fact they were trooping off to the towns.

The Municipal Reform Act of 1835 had affected only a limited number of towns, but the scheme of urban self-government was made general throughout England by the Local Government Act of 1888.

The legislators of 1835 had shirked the problem of the Capital: greater London, that is to say, all London outside the old City boundaries, had been left without unity of administration. Fifty years later, a bewildering chaos of overlapping authorities still carried on the affairs of the five million inhabitants of the Capital in haphazard fashion. The Local Government Act of 1888 applied a remedy long overdue. It established the London County Council, which has since governed London, all except the area of the ancient City, reserved as an historical monument under the Lord Mayor and Aldermen. Foreigners come to see the Lord Mayor, but the head of London's government is the Chairman of the London County Council.

The newborn London County Council sprang at once into vigorous life, and in the first twenty years of its existence carried out many new schemes of social welfare. And the London School Board during the same period made many leading experiments in education, till the Education Act of 1902 merged its activities in those of the London County Council. This forward move in local government by London, hitherto so backward, was conducted by the Progressive party that got the majority on the Council at one election after another. It called itself the *Progressive* party so as not to be completely identified with either the Liberal or the Labour party; but it had close affinities to both. It existed for municipal purposes only, and therefore people who voted Conservative at Parliamentary elections could vote Progressive at the County Council Election. The average London voter in the 'nineties was conservative and imperialist in national politics, but wanted democratic social improvement for himself and his City. It was in this atmosphere of a municipally progressive London that the Fabian Society flourished; the intellectual leadership of the Fabian publicists, the Sidney Webbs and Graham Wallas, had much to do with the Progressive government of London. But the popular leader was John Burns, who represented the coming alliance of Labour and Liberal. John Burns of Battersea was the first great apostle of a London patriotism, as distinct from pride in the 'City,' now shrunk within its ancient boundaries, a dignified memory of the past.

The towns, therefore, in the last decades of Victoria's reign were undergoing rapid improvement in sanitation, lighting, locomotion, public libraries and baths, and to some extent in housing. The example set in these matters by the Birmingham municipality under Joseph Chamberlain in the 'seventies, and by the London County Council twenty years later, was widely followed elsewhere. And the Central Government supported the efforts of the local authorities to better the life of the citizen by grants from taxes in aid of the local rates, conditional on favourable reports by Government Inspectors.

This movement of municipal reform supported by the State prevented an utter social catastrophe. The death-rate, so high in the early Victorian city, rapidly declined, town life was made increasingly tolerable on its purely material side, and primary education became universal. Nevertheless, it was in many respects a dreary heritage to pass on to the Twentieth Century. The modern city, in the unplanned swamp of its increase, lacks form and feature; it is a deadening cage for the human spirit. Urban and suburban life in modern England made no appeal through the eye to the imagination, as had the old village life of our island, or the city life of ancient and mediaeval Europe. Civic pride and civic rivalry among the industrial towns of the north was almost entirely materialistic and not at all aesthetic. The pall of smoke and smuts in itself was enough to discourage any effort after beauty or joy in the visible aspect of life.

The new cities were too big to have individual unity or character, or even to be seen by the eye as Athens, Rome, Perugia, Nuremberg, Tudor London and a thousand other older cities had been seen and loved. And to make matters worse there had been practically no town planning of the Victorian cities. The State had permitted the landlord and the speculative builder to lay out modern England as best suited their own private gain, too often without a thought given to amenity or to the public welfare. [See § 69.] In vast areas of London and other cities there were no open spaces within reach of the children, whose only playground outside the school yard was the hard and ugly street. To millions the divorce from nature was absolute, and so too was the divorce from all dignity and beauty and significance in the wilderness of mean streets in which they were bred, whether in the well-to-do suburb or the slum. The new education and the new journalism were both the outcome of these surroundings and partook of their nature. [See § 124.] The race bred under such conditions might retain many sturdy qualities of character, might even with better food and clothing improve in physique, might develop sharp wits and a brave, cheery, humorous attitude to life, but its imaginative powers must necessarily decline, and the stage is set for the gradual standardization of human personality.

The later Victorians, though incapable of coping with their own distress, were beginning to be aware of it. Ruskin had inspired the rising generations of writers and thinkers with disgust at the industrial civilization that had filled their fathers with such pride. Looking back through history, they thought they saw a fairer world than modern Lancashire; as early as 1868 William Morris, in the Prologue to *The Earthly Paradise*, had written:

> Forget six counties overhung with smoke,
> Forget the snorting steam and piston stroke,
> Forget the spreading of the hideous town;
> Think rather of the pack-horse on the down,
> And dream of London, small, and white and clean,
> The clear Thames bordered by its gardens green . . .

But there was no going back, except in imagination.

The year 1870 was a turning-point in educational and therefore in social history. Education was not only a national requirement on the necessity for which politicians were agreed; it was also the chief battleground of religious denominations. The main reason why English Education lagged behind in the mid-Victorian period was that no government, Whig or Tory, could conceive a means of setting up a national system at the public expense that would not have given the bitterest offence either to the Dissenters or to the Established Church. Until Gladstone's gallant venture in 1870, every government had shrunk from embarking on that sea of trouble. A network of Voluntary Schools paid for by private subscription had been spread over the country owing to religious and sectarian zeal; but the same zeal had frightened off both political parties from tackling the Education question as a national affair.

The great majority of the Voluntary Schools by which the primary education of the people was supplied, were conducted on Church principles: they were known as National Schools, because founded by the (Anglican) National Society. They had been aided by a very small grant since 1833. Gladstone's Bill of 1870 was the work of W. E. Forster, an ardent churchman though of Quaker origin. Forster's Bill doubled the State Grant to the existing Church Schools and to the Roman Catholic Schools so as to enable them to become a permanent part of the new system, while it introduced publicly controlled schools to fill up the large gaps in the educational map of the country. These new Schools, called Board Schools, were to be paid for out of the Local Rates, and they were to be governed by popularly elected School Boards. In most of the old Voluntary Schools, that is, in all National Schools, Church teaching was to be continued. But in the new Board Schools the Act prohibited the use, in the religious teaching, of catechism or formulary distinctive of any denomination.

The grievance of the Dissenters was that the State thus perpetuated the Church Schools of the villages, and in each village there was only one school available to which all children had to go. In the towns there were Board and Voluntary Schools side by side. It was unfortunate that the Church Schools were found most of all in the villages where there was no alternative school. That is so very largely to this day (1941), but it is less resented now than in 1870, partly because the hostile feeling between Church and Dissent has very much subsided, and partly because by Balfour's Act of 1902 the Church Schools have been brought under a considerable measure of control by County Councils as the public Educational Authorities.

By the religious compromise of 1870 England was enabled to obtain, better late than never, a system of universal primary education without which she must soon have fallen into the rear among modern nations. Between 1870 and 1890 the average school attendance rose from one and a quarter million to four and a half millions, while the money spent on each child was doubled. [See § 123, 124.]

But the State did little as yet for Secondary Education[1]; nor was there a sufficient ladder of school scholarships to the Universities

---

[1] 'In 1899 the amount of public money spent per head on Secondary Education was only three farthings in England, as compared with one shilling and a penny three farthings in Switzerland.' Bernard Allen's *Sir Robert Morant*, p. 141.

for the ablest children in Primary Schools. The new School Boards were charged with Primary Education only. In 1900 the Law Courts decided, in the famous Cockerton judgment, that the ratepayers' money could not be spent on any form of Secondary or Higher Education, under the terms of the Act of 1870.

Another defect in that measure was the smallness of the School Board areas. Each School Board being the affair of a single town or village could have no wide educational outlook. And their parochial character made the feud of Church and Dissent more personal and intense.

These defects in the Act of 1870 were remedied by Balfour's Education Act of 1902, inspired by the great public servant, Sir Robert Morant. This measure abolished School Boards and gave the power to provide for Education, both Primary and Secondary, to the elected County Councils, and to certain large Borough Councils. Such is our system to-day. The Councils do their educational work through their Education Committees. The improvement due to the larger area and broader views of these County Education Committees has been of great benefit to Primary Education, and of still greater benefit to Secondary Education; and an effective ladder to the Universities was created by Balfour's Bill.

Without the Education Acts of 1870 and of 1902 England could not have competed in the coming era of machinery and organization, and her people would have sunk into the barbarism of an uneducated city population, a far worse form of society than the uneducated rural population of old times, where the mind and character of ploughmen and craftsmen were formed by the influences of nature, the agricultural life and the old system of apprenticeship.

Our modern system of proper Education was indeed indispensable and has conferred great benefits on the country; but it has been a disappointment in some important respects. Being a town-made system it has failed to meet rural needs, of which the Board of Education failed to recognize the distinctive character. It has speeded up rather than diminished the rural exodus. More generally speaking, it has produced a vast population able to read but unable to distinguish what is worth reading, an easy prey to sensations and cheap appeals. Consequently both literature and journalism have been to a large extent debased since 1870, because they now cater for millions of half-educated and quarter-educated people, whose forbears, not being able to read at all, were not the patrons of newspapers or of books. The small highly educated class no longer sets the standards to the extent that it used to do, and tends to adopt the standards of the majority. Whether in the twentieth or twenty-first centuries the lower forms of literature and journalism will completely devour the higher has yet to be seen. If they do not, it will be due to improved Secondary and Higher Education forming a sufficiently large class to perpetuate a demand for things really worth reading.

The subject-matter of this book has been confined to the social history of England, and has not included the vast and varied expanse of lands beyond the ocean associated in the British Commonwealth of Nations and Dependencies. But social life in little England would have been a very different thing if it had not been the centre of a great maritime trade and, moreover, of an Empire. We had long prided ourselves on being a seafaring people; that was part of the island habit. But consciousness of the Empire, of which we had become the centre, lagged far behind the reality. In the middle of the Nineteenth Century popular patriotic songs still celebrated 'the right little, tight little island.' And that island was not yet generally thought of as the heart of 'an Empire on which the sun never set.' That aspect of our position was first fully appreciated at the two Jubilees of Queen Victoria (1887, 1897) when the pageant of distant and diverse lands, all come to pay homage to the little lady in grey, was first fully displayed, with startling effect, in London streets.

Yet, for generations past, the ways of thought and habits of life in English towns and villages had been strongly influenced by overseas connections. In the Eighteenth Century tea and tobacco had become as much the national food as beef and beer. And ever since the Seventeenth Century the adventurous and the discontented had been going across the ocean, first to the American colonies, then to the United States, to Canada, to Australia, to South Africa. It is true that until the Nineteenth Century the emigrant usually parted for ever from the folk he left behind and, however he fared, little more was heard of him. But in Victoria's reign, when the tide of emigration was still running stronger than ever, the postage stamp kept the cottage at home in touch with the son who had 'gone to the Colonies,' and often he would return on a visit with money in his pocket, and tales of new lands of equality and self-help and maybe an affectionate contempt for slow old ways at home. In this very human manner the middle and lower classes knew quite as much about the Empire as their 'betters,' and rather more than their 'betters' about the United States, as was shown at the time of the Civil War of 1861–1865. But the professional and upper classes also went out to careers all over the world, to govern, and trade, and shoot big game, in Africa and India. And all ranks of the army knew India, so far as it could be seen from the lines.

In this manner, a vast and varied overseas experience was for ever pouring back into every town and every hamlet in Victoria's England. Since Tudor times the influence of the sea had been strong even in upland villages, no one of which is more than seventy miles from a tidal estuary. And to the old maritime influence was now added in equally full measure the Colonial. Our island people were, in some respects, the least insular of all mankind. To Europeans we appeared insular, because we were not continental. But our experiences and opportunities were greater than those of the folk of other lands.

Victorian prosperity and Victorian civilization, alike in their grosser and their higher aspects, were due to a century's immunity from great wars and from any serious national danger. [See § 133, 134.] Safe behind the shield of the navy, Englishmen thought of all the problems of life in terms of peace and security which were in fact the outcome of temporary and local circumstances, and not part of nature's universal order. [See § 130.] No great country except English-speaking America has ever been so utterly civilian in thought and practice as Victorian England. Service in the army was regarded by the middle and working classes as disgraceful—except in time of war.

It's Tommy this and Tommy that, an' 'Chuck him out, the brute!'
But it's 'Saviour of 'is country,' when the guns begin to shoot.

It was a vulgar attitude, especially as it went with occasional fits of Jingoism like those which preceded the Crimean and Boer Wars, and nearly caused several others. But for a hundred years after Trafalgar and Waterloo it led to no fatal results. For we held the surface of the sea, and the surface was then all the sea for human action. On the whole our supremacy in the oceans and along the shores of the world was used in the Nineteenth Century on the side of peace, goodwill and freedom. If it were to be destroyed, mankind would breathe a harsher air.

The carefree Victorians knew little about the spirit and inner workings of the militarized continent, off which this green and happy isle was anchored. They knew more about Australia, America, Africa in a human and business way. Europe was the Englishman's playground, with its Alps, its picture galleries, its ancient cities. We were islanders with an overseas Empire, not continentals. We were sailors not soldiers. We thought of European politics not in terms of power or of our own national security, but according as we liked or disliked the governments of Turkey or Russia, Napoleon III or the Italian *risorgimento*. Sometimes these sympathies led us right, sometimes wrong. But in any case there could be no consistent national policy with armaments adapted to it. To the Englishman, foreign affairs were a branch of Liberal and Conservative politics, tinged with emotion, a matter of taste, not a question of existence.

In the Victorian era this attitude could be indulged without disaster. But when the reign and the Century came to an end, a tremendous revolution in all human affairs was imminent. The internal combustion engine had been invented, and its space-annihilating consequences were about to be disclosed. The motor-car and motor-lorry, the submarine, the tank, the aeroplane were about to plunge the world into a new era, widely different from the past in peace and in war. [See § 128, 129.] And England would be the country most concerned of all, because she would lose half the benefit of her insular position. The surface of the sea could no longer be held by ships alone; and whether it was held or not, the aeroplane could violate the thousand-year-old sanctities of the peaceful island. In such new conditions our happy-go-lucky attitude towards power on the Continent, and our wholly civilian way of life, our refusal to arm ourselves adequately to new needs, if continued too long, might become a terrible danger.

And even in peacetime the new age of motor traction on the roads made a more rapid social and economic revolution in the first forty years of the Twentieth Century than railways and machinery had made before. In the age of the railway, supplemented by horse traffic and bicycles, the pace of changes, the disappearance of local and provincial differences though rapid, was limited. But under the new conditions England bade fair to become one huge unplanned suburb. Motor traction created the urgent need for the State to control the development of the whole island, but unhappily the matter was left to chance and the building exploiter. Political society could not at once adjust its habits of thought to new conditions coming on with unexampled speed.

But there are good points in this latest age. The progress actually made in the first forty years of the new Century, particularly in education[1] and in social services, has perhaps been as much as can be expected of limited human wisdom. The material conditions of the working class in 1939 were much better than in the year Queen Victoria died.

What will now happen to England in peace and in war the historian is no better able to guess than anyone else. And the tremendous changes that have already taken place in the first forty years of the new Century will no doubt, a short time hence, look different from what they now appear, and will fall into a new historical perspective. The best place, therefore, to bring to an end a social history of England is the death of Queen Victoria and the end of the railway age. [See § 135.]

---

[1] The battle of Waterloo was won, not on the playing fields of Eton, but on the village greens of England. The men who fought in the ranks on June 18, 1815, were little educated but they had the qualities of countrybred men. To-day we are urban and educated. The flyers of the R.A.F. are not and could not be the product of rural simplicity. If we win this war, it will have been won in the primary and secondary schools (1941).

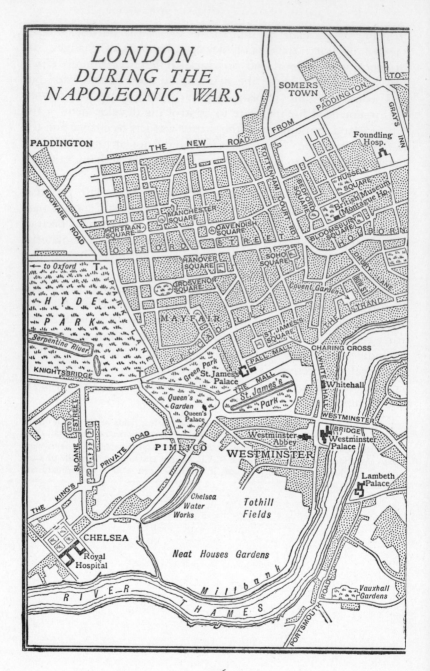

LONDON
DURING THE
NAPOLEONIC WARS

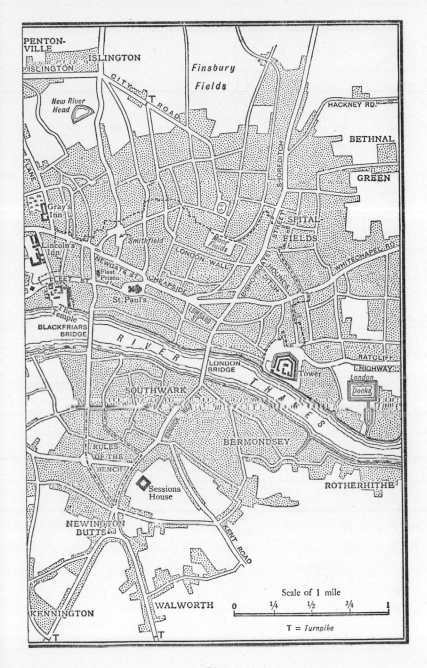

PENTON-
VILLE
ISLINGTON          ISLINGTON

New River
Head                          Finsbury
                              Fields
                                                    HACKNEY RD.

CITY        ROAD        T                    BETHNAL

                                             GREEN

                              SHOREDITCH
Gray's
Inn                                          SPITAL
                                   Moor       FIELDS
Lincoln's           Smithfield    fields
Inn                                          BISHOPSGATE    WHITECHAPEL RD.
        NEWGATE ST.   LONDON WALL
FLEET ST. Fleet    CHEAPSIDE
The      Prison
Temple          St. Paul's    LOMBARD
BLACKFRIARS
BRIDGE                                                       RATCLIFF
                    RIVER                                    HIGHWAY
                              LONDON        Tower      London
                              BRIDGE                   Docks
        SOUTHWARK             THAMES

                                                            London
RULES                                                       Docks
OF THE                        BERMONDSEY
BENCH
                                                     ROTHERHITHE
        Sessions
        House

NEWINGTON
BUTTS
                                                   Scale of 1 mile
                          KENT ROAD
                                        0    ¼    ½    ¾    1
KENNINGTON      WALWORTH
                                        T = Turnpike
T           T

127

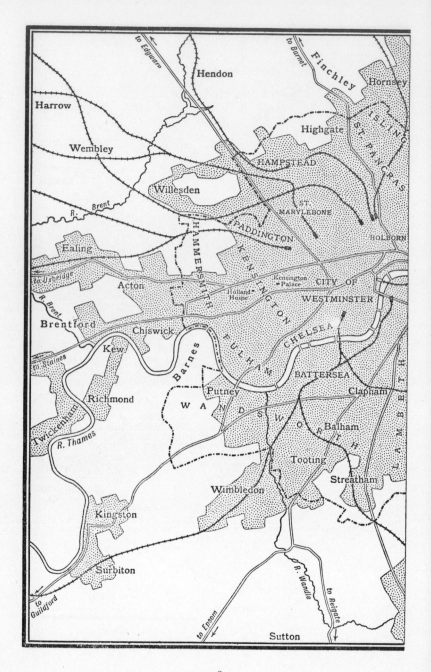

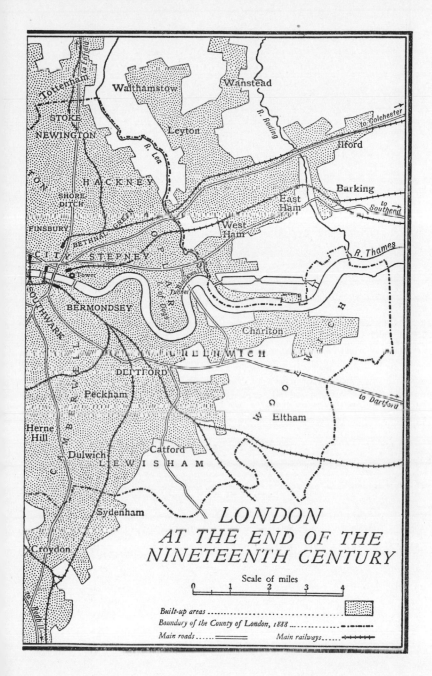

LONDON
*AT THE END OF THE*
*NINETEENTH CENTURY*

Scale of miles

0    1    2    3    4

Built-up areas ..............................................
Boundary of the County of London, 1888 .............
Main roads .......... Main railways ....←←←←←

# DESCRIPTIVE NOTES
## TO THE ILLUSTRATIONS

These are grouped into three categories : 1. Colour Plates ; 2. Gravure Plates (marked §) ; 3. Illustrations in the text

Colour Plate I  *Frontispiece* (cf. text p. 41)

Fox Hunting. From a colour engraving by Samuel Howett in *British Field Sports*, published by Edward Orme (1807). From the copy in the Department of Printed Books, British Museum. (Cf. notes to § 43 and 44).

Both this illustration and Colour Plate II are reproduced here principally as examples of the coloured books and prints of the time rather than for their subject matter, though this scene of fox hunting in the early XIXth century might be compared with similar scenes in earlier centuries to underline the unchanging pattern of sport and country life, in spite of changing fashions and ideas. (Cf. the XVIIth century scenes in Vol. II, § 106–111, and the XVIIIth century hunt in Vol. III, § 117).

Colour Plate II (cf. text p. 40)

Clare Hall Piece and the New Buildings of King's College, Cambridge. Coloured lithograph from Rudolph Ackermann's *History of the University of Cambridge* (1815).

The German, Rudolph Ackermann, who set up his print shop in the Strand in 1795, was responsible for a whole series of illustrated works, ranging from *The Repository of Arts*, etc. (cf. § 4 and 5), and the *Microcosm of London* (§ 31), to his histories of the universities and of public schools (cf. § 45–48).

This illustration shows the gate of Clare College (Clare Hall as it was until 1856) in the foreground, and across the wide lawns the Gibbs building of King's, planned in 1723 by James Gibbs as part of a new quadrangle, a scheme which was never carried out in its entirety. (Cf. note to Colour Plate I above.)

Colour Plate III (cf. text p. 61)

Queen Victoria's sitting room at Balmoral (1857). From a chromolithograph (after the painting by J. Roberts) in *Leaves from the Journal of our Life in the Highlands (1848–61)*. Illustrated edition (1868), edited by Arthur Helps. (Cf. note to § 57.)

Queen Victoria wished to model the rooms at Balmoral on the cottage rather than the palace and the simplicity and freshness of this picture of her sitting room in the autumn of 1857 should be compared with that of the Prince Consort (§ 57).

Colour Plate IV (cf. text p. 70)

Bus Interior. From the original painting by William Egley (1859) in the Tate Gallery, London. (By courtesy of the Trustees.) This painting of the interior of a horse bus with its closely packed and varied load of passengers gives an excitingly real glimpse of mid Victorian everyday life and people. William Egley (probably the son of W. Maw Egley the miniaturist) exhibited from 1843 to 1898; his richness of colour and meticulous detail proclaim him an adherent of the Pre-Raphaelites. Other illustrations of horse buses in this volume are § 76, 129 and 133. The first omnibus service is said to have been initiated by Louis XIVth in the Paris of 1662; but three-horse buses appeared in London in 1829, introduced by a certain Shillibeer —a coach proprietor. These gave way later in the century to two-horse buses, which had for outside passengers seating, reached by a ladder. The outside seat ran lengthways and was known as the knife-board, the passengers sitting back to back as in an Irish jaunting car.

§ 1 (cf. text p. 4)

William Cobbett. From the portrait by an unknown artist in the National Portrait Gallery.

William Cobbett (1762–1835), ploughman, soldier, pugnacious reformer, politician, journalist and farmer, was a self-educated man, the vigorous mouthpiece of popular reform, the irrepressible upholder of the poor and oppressed. His *Rural Rides* show him at his most characteristic, full of violent prejudices, imbued with the love of imparting information, strongly individual, sharply observant, contemptuous of stupidity, childishly delighted wherever he could see the agricultural methods he himself approved being applied. But in spite of all his radical sound and fury the core of his beliefs was reactionary enough, his tastes feudal rather than new-fangled. The squandering of public money was a special object of his invective, the building of a martello tower was in his eyes so many labourers' cottages the less—a success for the hated stock jobber and war profiteer at the expense of agricultural prosperity.

He is strongly typical of his age in savage hard hitting, in seeing things in harsh black and white, and in translating impersonal issues into personal terms: for which characteristics there is some parallel in the spirit of Gillray's caricatures of the Napoleonic wars (cf. § 2 and 3).

§ 2 (cf. text pp. 5, 34)

'Fighting for the Dunghill or Jack Tar settling Buonaparte.' Political satire by James Gillray (20 November 1798) from Bohn's edition of Gillray's collected works (1851). From a copy in the Cambridge University Library.

Jack Tar is here represented by Gillray as full of fight and confident of 'settling' Boney, but it should be remembered that the Navy at this time was in a far from healthy condition: the mutinies at the Nore and Spithead were fresh in men's memories from the year before, but Nelson's resounding victory over the French fleet at the Battle of the Nile in the August of 1798 was fresher still. The English sailor held himself free to rebel against the evil conditions obtaining for food and creature comforts, pay and punishment, while at the same time he was ready to put up a splendid fight against the foreigner when necessary (cf. text p. 34).

§ 3 (cf. text p. 4)

'John Bull's Progress.' Political satire by James Gillray (3 June 1793) from Bohn's edition of Gillray's collected works (1851). From a copy in the Department of Prints and Drawings, British Museum.

This series of four scenes shows in succession John Bull prosperous in peacetime, John Bull going off to the wars, the plight of his family during his absence, and his return—crippled, blinded and ragged—to his starving and destitute family. It was all too common a story during the long struggle with France and may be compared with the similar story depicted by Grimm twenty-three years before (cf. § 48 in Volume III) though in very different mood.

§ 4 and 5 (cf. text p. 4)

The Temple of the Muses, Finsbury Square, and Messrs. Harding, Howell and Co.'s shop in Pall Mall. From Rudolph Ackermann's *Repository of the Arts*, etc. (1809). From a copy in the Department of Printed Books, British Museum.

That life's amenities were obtainable in England much as usual during the time of war and upheaval in Europe is implied by these two illustrations. The first shows James Lackington's famous bookshop 'The Temple of the Muses,' said to have been the largest in London; the second shows the draper's establishment of Messrs. Harding, Howell and Co. at 89 Pall

Mall (that is, where the Royal Automobile Club stands to-day). Both might serve as illustrations to Jane Austen's novels, allowing but for the larger scale and higher fashion of the metropolis. Here might Isabella Thorpe have asked for 'Udolpho' or 'The Necromancer of the Black Forest,' or Catherine Morland have chosen 'the spotted, the sprigged, the mull or the jackonet.'

§ 6, 7 and 8 (cf. text p. 4)

§ 6 Sir Walter Scott. From the painting by Landseer (1824) in the National Portrait Gallery.

Walter Scott (1771–1832) is illustrated here as the exponent of the romanticism of history, the teller of tales of old, the preserver of ballads, the singer of minstrels and ladies and lords of the isles—antiquary, novelist and poet.

A friend of Wordsworth, he represented another facet of the romanticism of this great period of English writing.

§ 7 William Wordsworth. From the portrait by B. R. Haydon (1842) in the National Portrait Gallery.

This portrait of Wordsworth (1770–1850) is a late one showing the mature poet and thinker against his own lakeland rocks; but Wordsworth, first the poet of political liberty and later of poetical liberty in form and subject, is predominantly the singer of the new-found delight in natural beauty, especially of lakes and mountains, but also of 'sylvan combes' and flowery meadows, though to him they meant more than purely visual beauty for

> Early had he learned
> To reverence the volume that displays
> The mystery, the life which cannot die;
> But in the mountains did he *feel* his faith;
> All things, responsive to the writing, there
> Breathed immortality, revolving life
> And greatness still revolving, infinite: . . .
>
> (*Excursion*, Bk. I, 223 f.)

§ 8 Crossing the Brook. From the original painting by Turner (1813–15) in the National Gallery.

This was the great age of poetry in romantic landscape as well as in verse.

Such a painter as Richard Wilson (strongly influenced by Claude) had already produced scenes of river and mountain, of lakes and castles, with Italianate trees and green and golden evening skies, while the romantic exaggeration of English hills to rival Alpine heights was also well established in the later

XVIIIth century in the work, for instance, of Joseph Farington and would continue into the middle of the XIXth with such a painter as Charles Barber. It remained for Turner, however, before the full flowering of his genius in the pictorial treatment of light and atmosphere, to provide the visual counterpart in painting to the romanticism of the poets of his time.

This picture shows the valley of the Tamar, looking down towards Plymouth, with Calstock Bridge; to poets and painters alike 'meadow, grove and stream, the earth and every common sight' appeared 'apparelled in celestial light; the glory and the freshness of a dream.'

§ 9, 10, 11 and 12 (cf. text pp. 15, 20)

The Wensley Dale Knitters, the Cloth Dressers, the Factory Children and the Sheffield Cutler. From *The Costume of Yorkshire* edited (with facsimile plates executed by Ernst Kaufmann from George Walker's original paintings of 1814) by Edward Hailstone (1885). From a copy in the Department of Printed Books, British Museum.

George Walker (1781–1856) came of a family of drysalters of Leeds, but himself took up the study of natural history and the fine arts. He sketched Yorkshire scenery and founded an exhibition at Leeds named 'The Northern Exhibition of Paintings.' He was an intimate friend of Charles Waterton, the eccentric squire of Walton Hall.

These sketches are somewhat crude in execution and colour (judging from the facsimile plates published) but their main interest lies in their faithful intention to depict the customs and dress of a limited area. The editor (Edward Hailstone) possessed George Walker's original paintings and was at pains to provide local information to explain and supplement those he published.

§ 9 The Wensley Dale Knitters (we are told) resort to knitting in any business where they do not require to use their hands, for instance, shepherds watching their flocks, men driving cattle, women going to market. The editor mentions one woman who in this way accomplished a complete pair of men's stockings per day, knitting on her way to market, while she superintended her goods there, and on her homeward journey. Such rural and unorganized industry existed side by side with such activities as

§ 10 'cropping' or cloth dressing, where the process represented only part of an industry. 'Cropping' the wool of the cloth was done by wetting the cloth thoroughly in a cistern, then combing the wool with teazles in a wooden frame, drying and brushing the cloth on tenters, placing on a shear board and clipping (as in the illustration). The 'cropper' supported the handle of the shears on one hand, and worked them with a small lever or gig fixed to the upper edge. We are told that many croppers came from the west of England or Ireland: they were regarded as unsteady labour, and because of this employers are said to have welcomed the invention of gig mills and shearing frames, as eliminating the loss and inconvenience suffered by them under the old method.

§ 11 Factory children—illustrates two of these stunted small employees (with the mill that employed them in the background). The West Riding of Yorkshire had many cloth 'manufactories,' 'now' (the writer notes) 'usually known under the general, though perhaps vulgar, denomination of Factories.' While claiming that these provided the means of employment, food and clothing for many thousands 'of poor industrious individuals,' the editor admits that this was frequently at the expense of health and morals, but that many proprietors of factories had tried to remedy these evils by strict attention to the morals, behaviour and cleanliness of the children and by 'adopting a plan of consuming or burning the smoke.' (Cf. Volume III, note to § 64 on child labour conditions: also § 93 and § 94 and note in the present volume.)

§ 12 The Sheffield Cutler is illustrated here, not so much as to give details of how the cutlery trade actually worked, but rather as an indication that it was already well established as a leading Yorkshire industry. The cutler is shown just finishing a knife.

§ 13 (cf. text p. 8)

'The Lord of the Manor receiving his rents.' From a water-colour drawing by Thomas Rowlandson in the collection of Gilbert Davis, Esq.

The gouty greedy landlord, his skinflint steward and his equally unprepossessing tenantry are none of them spared the sting of Rowlandson's satire. The caricaturist draws on the extreme to make his point and we may contrast this sketch with the next illustration, where Rowlandson in another mood depicts a jolly farmer and his even jollier labourers bringing home the harvest.

§ 14 (cf. text pp. 10, 13)

'Harvest Home.' From the coloured etching by Thomas Rowlandson for *The Third Tour of Doctor Syntax in Search of a*

*Wife* (published by Rudolph Ackermann 1821). From a copy in the Department of Printed Books, British Museum.

That Rowlandson could turn readily from depicting, in a mood of biting sarcasm, the miserly landlord and beggarly tenants of the preceding illustration, to a facile and idyllic representation of bucolic merrymaking, is shown by this harvest home, where a jolly farmer leads home his rejoicing peasantry with dance and song followed by high piled wains drawn by sturdy oxen. These peasants we feel have never needed to heed the grim game laws affixed to the wall in § 13.

§ 15 (cf. text p. 12)

The Collier. From *The Costume of Yorkshire*, edited (with facsimile plates by Ernst Kaufmann from George Walker's original paintings of 1814) by Edward Hailstone (1885). From the copy in the Department of Printed Books, British Museum. (For a general note on George Walker cf. note to § 9–12 above.) The Yorkshire collier (we are told by the editor of *The Costume of Yorkshire*) wore a dress of white cloth bound with red, to facilitate frequent washing. In the background can be seen the mine workings and a steam engine 'lately invented by Mr. Blenkinsop, agent at the colliery of Charles Brindling, near Leeds,' which drew twenty waggons from the pit to Leeds. (For a note on early steam engines and the forerunner of the railway cf. note to § 85 below.) (For mining scenes cf. § 16 and 17.)

§ 16 and § 17 (cf. text p. 12)

Crane for loading the rollies and the Church Pit at Wallsend. From *Sketches of the coal mines in Northumberland and Durham*, by T. H. Hair (1844), with descriptive sketches by M. Ross. From a copy in the Department of Printed Books, British Museum. These two illustrations of scenes down a coal mine and at the pit-head date from some thirty years later than that of the collier in § 15. The publisher, in his preface to the book from which they are drawn, thinks it necessary to excuse himself for the subject of it because of the importance of the coal mines to the national economy, although some may regard it with apathy in view of the 'apparently unpromising nature of the subject.'

§ 16 shows miners with a pit pony in an underground gallery. Small waggons—'trams'—contain the baskets of coal, which are dragged along the 'rolly ways' to the bottom of the shaft.

§ 17 shows the pit-head. On rails in the foreground a waggon filled with coal moves forward on a gentle incline, impelled by one man's push-off. Another railroad from another colliery crosses this (numerous intersections of this kind covered the whole district from one colliery to another). In the centre is the 'shaft frame' supporting the pulleys by which the men were lowered into the pit. The brick chimney (or funnel) near it has a smoke disperser at the top to dispel the impure air; on the right is the engine house. (Cf. § 17 with § 63 in Volume III.)

§ 18 and 19 (cf. text p. 15)

The Servants' Registry (1802) and the Servants' Dinner (1806). From water-colour drawings by Thomas Rowlandson in the collection of Gilbert Davis, Esq.

In this sketch of 'the only reputable office in London' Rowlandson knows how to extract the maximum fun from the raw youth on the left being interviewed by the lady with the feather, to the beau quizzing the demure damsel by the window or the elderly roué in the foreground looking for a pretty young parlour maid and closely observed by the fat cook on the right. In the scene of the servants' dinner, Rowlandson shows us a vast kitchen with a roaring fire, before which is turning a round of beef; the walls and dresser reveal rows of shining covers, dishes and plates; hams are curing from the ceiling and at the table gathers a well-fed throng of servants; the cook with her assistants is busy on the right and two men servants hurry out with covered dishes for 'upstairs.'

§ 20 (cf. text p. 15)

Three Locks, Stoke Hammond, Bucks. From an engraving in *Tour of the Grand Junction Canal* by John Hassall (1819). From a copy in the Department of Printed Books, British Museum.

The as yet unspoiled rural character of the country bordering a canal in 1819 with the lock keeper's cottage like any other countryman's dwelling, may be contrasted with § 21, which shows the permanent change effected in the scene, when a railway came to be built; even though an army of 'navvies' would necessarily have been employed to cut the canal.

§ 21 (cf. text p. 15)

Entrance to the tunnel of the Liverpool and Manchester Railway at Edge Hill. From an engraving (after C. and G. Pyne) in *Lancashire Illustrated* (1831) by W. H. Pyne. From a copy in the Cambridge University Library.

The Liverpool and Manchester Railway begun in 1826 was opened in 1830, and really established the supremacy of the steam locomotive, though the Stockton and Darlington Railway had been opened five years earlier. (Cf. § 85 and note.) A separate note on railway development will be found under that for § 85, but this illustration is given here to show 'navvies' in action constructing tunnel and embankment, and to emphasize the permanent change effected in the countryside by the railway, as distinct from the slighter change brought about by canal development. (Cf. § 20 and note.)

§ 22 (cf. text p. 21)

'A view of the agricultural and manufacturing villages of Unity and Mutual Co-operation' from the woodcut in *The Times* of 9 August 1817. This plan accompanied Mr. Robert Owen's report to the Committee of the House of Commons on the Poor Laws in the session of 1817.

Robert Owen (1771–1858) is chiefly remembered for his experiment at New Lanark Mills on the principle that good work could only be expected from well-fed, well-clothed and educated workers. With the aid of Jeremy Bentham his mills were converted into a workers' trust (1814) and institutions 'for the formation of character' were opened as schools two years later. By 1817 he had put forward these schemes for villages of unity and mutual co-operation; the woodcut given here exhibits an amazingly early attempt at planning an industrial unit with an appropriate amount of land to go with it. It consisted of the mill itself, standing by itself in an open plot of ground, while a short distance away the workers' living quarters are shown enclosing a square with gardens and public buildings in the centre. In the distance another similar village is depicted.

One settlement was established at Orbiston in Lanarkshire and lasted about two years, involving Owen in great financial loss. He then established another in 1825 at New Harmony in Indiana, but by 1828 this also was abandoned, since he found himself powerless to enforce the principles upon which he had based it. In the following year he also withdrew from the New Lanark Mills set-up entirely, having quarrelled with his partners; from then on he devoted himself to theory and lecturing, and to attendance at co-operative and social science congresses. The co-operative movement proper started in 1844 with the establishment of the Pioneer Society in Rochdale.

§ 23 (cf. text p. 22)

The 'Lowkers' from *The Costume of Yorkshire*, edited (with facsimile plates executed by Ernst Kaufmann from George Walker's original paintings of 1814) by Edward Hailstone (1885). From the copy in the Department of Printed Books, British

Museum. (For a general note on George Walker, cf. note to § 9–12 above.)

'This garrulous class of mortals,' as the editor of *The Costume of Yorkshire* calls the 'lowkers' was made up chiefly of old women and children employed in spring to weed out the young corn. The work was carried out by hand with tools such as a 'grub' (for thistles) held by the woman in front. The usual tool was the 'clam,' nippers on a long handle, to be seen to the right of the plate. In the background is the owner of the field on horseback to overlook the workers.

§ 24 (cf. text p. 24)

'A Modern Belle going to the Rooms at Bath.' Social satire by James Gillray (13 January 1796). From Bohn's edition of Gillray's collected works (1851). From a copy in the Cambridge University Library.

An ingenious (if satirical) solution, showing how the monstrous head-dresses worn at this period might be accommodated in a sedan chair.

§ 25 (cf. text p. 24).

'Dr. Syntax with a Bluestocking Beauty.' From the coloured etching by Thomas Rowlandson in *The Third Tour of Doctor Syntax in Search of a Wife*. Published by Rudolph Ackermann (1821). From a copy in the Department of Printed Books, British Museum.

Madam Omicron, a bluestocking beauty, visited by Dr. Syntax in his search for a wife, is pictured by Rowlandson as turbaned and languid in an extensive and well-stocked library. She seems to be about to write down some ideas that have just occurred to her and which make her press her brow, rather than to be listening to the learned doctor.

The term 'bluestocking' had become familiar about the middle of the XVIIIth century to denote women (such as Mrs. Elizabeth Montague) who met together to discuss literary subjects; these assemblies at first included men members but later became confined to women only. Rowlandson's bluestocking beauty was a 'poseur' and illustrated a wealthy widow, with little to do, masquerading as a bluestocking, rather than the genuinely learned woman that the term usually denoted.

§ 26 (cf. text p. 24)

'Dr. Syntax at a Card Party.' From a coloured etching by Thomas Rowlandson in *The Third Tour of Doctor Syntax in Search of a Wife*. Published by Rudolph Ackermann (1821).

From a copy in the Department of Printed Books, British Museum.

His travels in search of a wife brought Dr. Syntax to Lady Macnight (a cousin of Squire Hearty) and here he can be seen playing Pope Joan with her and her neighbours. His next-door neighbour at table proposed 'to share the gain and loss with him,' which needless to say benefited the dame at the expense of the doctor.

§ 27 (cf. text p. 26)

'Farmer Giles and his Wife, showing off their Daughter Betty to their Neighbours on her return from School.' Social satire by James Gillray (1 January 1809) From Bohn's edition of Gillray's collected works (1851). From a copy in the Cambridge University Library.

Gillray here makes uproarious fun of the English farmers who sought 'to ape their betters' (cf. text p. 9) and had their daughters taught accomplishments, which certainly could not fit them for their future roles as farmers' wives and daughters.

§ 28 (cf. text p. 40)

'Very Slippy Weather.' From a satire by James Gillray in Bohn's edition of Gillray's collected works (1851). From a copy in the Cambridge University Library.

Gillray here shows the shop of his publisher, Mrs. Humphrey, in St. James's Street. In the bow window with its small panes can be seen the coloured cartoons which always attracted a crowd of gazers. Among the subjects can be recognized many of Gillray's most well-known prints.

§ 29 and 30 (cf. text p. 28)

'Characters on the Steyne at Brighton' and 'Evening Party in the Yellow Room at the Pavilion, Brighton.' From coloured prints by Robert Cruikshank and G. M. Brighty in The English Spy, by Bernard Blackmantle (C. M. Westmacott) (1825–6). From a copy in the Cambridge University Library.

Pierce Egan's Life in London had appeared in 1821 with coloured etchings by the two Cruikshanks and was quickly imitated by others, since the adventures of Corinthian Tom, Bob Logic and Jerry Hawthorn were an immediate success. The English Spy (from which these illustrations are drawn) was of this type: its author practised a kind of journalistic blackmail and his scandalous anecdotes got him into trouble more than once. The English Spy contains many of the celebrities of the day, Pierce Egan himself, the authority on all forms of sport and slang, among them. The book describes life in London, at Eton and the Universities and at popular resorts such as Brighton.

§ 29 shows the Steyne, the beach and the chain pier, and Westmacott notes with displeasure how 'the great advantages of expeditious travelling enable the multitudinous population of London to pour forth its motley groups.' Westmacott corroborates Cobbett in describing how the stockjobbers rush down to Brighton directly the Stock Exchange closes, though he claims that more speculations are carried out on the Saturday there than all the week before in London. The big wheel (to be seen in front of the chain pier) was for throwing up water for the use of the town. Note the Regency terrace, the verandahs and balconies giving their characteristic line.

§ 30 purports to illustrate an evening party in the Pavilion. The Yellow Drawing Room is shown hung with fluted drapery of yellow satin representing a Chinese tent, the chandelier of many-coloured glass, the chimney-piece also 'Chinese,' the stove 'formed by chimera chased in ormulu,' while the ottomans are of yellow velvet. George IV is shown with the Princess Augusta and the Duke of York in the foreground, the figure on crutches is the Earl of Arran, others of the party being the Marquis and Marchioness of Conyngham, and the Earl and Countess of Warwick.

Robert (1789–1856) and George (1792–1878) Cruikshank, sons of Isaac Cruikshank, the caricaturist, were both book illustrators and caricaturists, particularly of London life and humour. Other examples of their work are reproduced in § 35, 37, 38, 41, 76 and 77; their caricatures show a satirical flavour, nearer to Hogarth's, than that of either Leech or Doyle.

§ 31 (cf. text p. 33)

The West India Docks. From a coloured etching in the *Microcosm of London*. Published by Rudolph Ackermann (1808–11). From a copy in the Cambridge University Library.

Augustus Pugin and Thomas Rowlandson collaborated to illustrate the *Microcosm*. The former was responsible for the architectural part of the views, the latter for the figures. The text was designed to give with the plates a panorama of London life and London buildings. This is chosen to show a scene in London's docks, with a close line of merchant ships to emphasize the source of London's commercial wealth and prosperity. The West India Docks were designed to receive all shipping of the Port of London engaged in the West India trade and were projected by a West India merchant, Robert Milligan, in 1800.

§ 32 and 33 (cf. text pp. 34, 35)

Life in the Navy. From coloured etchings by Thomas Rowlandson in *The Adventures of Johnny Newcome in the Navy*, by Alfred Burton (1818). From a copy in the Cambridge University Library.

This book tells the story of a 'Johnny Raw's' experiences as a midshipman. With his father he dines on his first night with the Captain and two Lieutenants (or 'Luffs') but when his father returns to shore the fun begins. On going below to his allotted quarters he finds his hammock ready slung for him; he tries to emulate his companions' easy vaulting, but 'flew clean over t'other side' and sensibly 'to guard against a second wreck, he spread his mattress on the deck' but this did not solve his troubles, for the midshipmen above with fish-hook and line drew his mattress out from under him, until he proved his mettle by punching his tormentors' noses. The rest of the narrative describes all the troubles that could befall a greenhorn on a man o' war.

§ 34 (cf. text p. 38)

'Road to a Fight.' From colour prints by Henry Alken in *Real Life in London*, by an Amateur (1821). From a copy in the Department of Printed Books, British Museum.

*Real Life in London* tells the adventures of Tom Dashall and Bob Tallyho. This illustration shows the scene on the roads when they went to see 'a pugilistic encounter' or 'milling match' between Jack Randall 'the Nonpareil' and Martin 'the Master of the Rolls.' Piccadilly was jammed with 'coaches, carts, gigs, tilburies, whiskies, buggies, dogcarts, sociables, dunnets, curricles and sulkies' intermingled with tax-carts and waggons decorated with laurel. On their way their barouche passes all kinds of broken-down vehicles, overtaking numerous pedestrians and horsemen. 'The public-houses were thronged to excess, and the Turnpike keepers made a market of the mirth-moving throng.'

They arrived at Copthorne at half-past twelve and found the fight was to take place in Farmer Jarvis's meadow. Here the ring was formed and all the motley mass of vehicles admitted— 'proper contributions' being levied; however some gentlemen objected that the sacredness of their fences was not being maintained, and insisted on removal to Crawley Downs. The move took place accordingly (with much confusion and bad feeling); further delay followed since one pugilist insisted on taking his stand in Jarvis's meadow and the other on Crawley Downs. However, at twenty minutes to three the fight eventually began at the latter place to last only seven and a half minutes in all. A second fight provided an hour's contest, but the amusement was destroyed by a large gang of pickpockets and it being late Dashall and Tallyho set off back to Town, finding the roads as much clogged as they had been in the morning. (Cf. § 35 and 36 and notes thereto.)

§ 35 (cf. text p. 39).

Tom Cribb. From a colour print by I. R. and G. Cruikshank in Pierce Egan's *Life in London* (1821). From a copy in the Cambridge University Library.

*Life in London* tells ·the adventures of Corinthian Tom, Jerry Hawthorn and Bob Logic and 'their rambles and sprees through the Metropolis.' (Cf. note to § 29 and 30.) Bob and Jerry were introduced by Tom to Tom Cribb the Champion, whose parlour was filled with numerous portraits and other sporting subjects. 'The room' (says Egan) 'speaks for itself—it can be seen at all times, and therefore it may be identified when any person thinks proper. The Champion was blowing a cloud, always happy and contented—and had just taken off those Jack Boots, which stand at the bottom of the table and which weigh twenty pounds.' The silver cup (in Tom's hands) had been presented to Cribb by the Sporting World on 2 December 1811 with a complimentary address on his prowess, and manly and upright conduct. (For general note on the Cruikshanks cf. note to § 29 and 30.)

§ 36 (cf. text p. 39)

The Ring. From a coloured print by Henry Alken in *Real Life in London*, by an Amateur (1821). From a copy in the Department of Printed Books, British Museum.

As distinct from the kind of prize-fight which took place out of town (as described in the note to § 34) there were also 'exhibitions' such as that of Fives Court, which took place in London itself. Prize-fighting is said to have been first established as a public entertainment at the Dorset Gardens Theatre in 1698. Prize-fights (or 'mills') took place either on a grassy space, the spectators forming a 'ring' (cf. § 34) or on a raised wooden platform roped round to form the ring (as in this illustration). Many champion prize-fighters had their own amphitheatre where they staged sparring exhibitions or schools where the art of self-defence was taught.

The game of 'fives' was very popular in the early XIXth century and was played on tennis courts or small enclosed areas specially built for the purpose as this one in our illustration appears to have been. Two famous fives courts were by St. Martins-in-the-Fields and Leicester Fields; such a court could be used for ball games such as fives or racquets or easily converted to enable sparring exhibitions to be held as here. It is perhaps worth noting that James Belcher, the famous pugilist, lost an eye at racquets.

§ 37 and 38 (cf. text p. 39)

The St. Leger at Doncaster and Tattersall's. From colour prints by Robert Cruikshank in *The English Spy*, by Bernard Black-mantle (C. M. Westmacott) (1825–6). From a copy in the Cambridge University Library. (For a general note on *The English Spy* cf. note § 29 and 30.)

'The humorous description' which accompanies this plate of the Great St. Leger of 1825 does not afford much information on the meeting, but the text relating to that of 'Monday after the Great St. Leger' at Tattersall's (even though it is Monday after the St. Leger of 1823 and not of the one shown in § 37), when Bob Transit (i.e. Cruikshank) sketched it on the spot, affords more local colour. Monday was the 'settling' day for all the bets made on the race 'a noble opportunity for a picture of turf curiosities.' Here in short is Tattersall's 'whether for buying a good horse, betting a round sum or, in the sporting phrase, "learning how to make the best of everything."' Here may be found the jockey persuading his patron (a young blood) into a good thing; the poker-faced betting man proper, who can lose and pay without moving a muscle; the sporting earls, or generals and lawyers; the touts and spongers. (Cf. § 82 and 83 for a Victorian racing scene.)

The St. Leger race was founded by Colonel St. Leger of Park-hill, Doncaster, in 1776, while Tattersall's was established in 1766 near Hyde Park Corner and combined an auction room for race horses and subscription rooms; its founder was Richard Tattersall, who had been a stud groom to the Duke of Kingston. It was not moved to Knightsbridge until 1865, when a sub-scription room was reserved for Jockey Club members; Tattersall's was a centre for bookmakers and backers and the weekly settlement of bets took place there. (For general note on the Cruikshanks cf. note to § 29 and 30.)

§ 39 (cf. text p. 41)

The Road. From a coloured etching by Thomas Rowlandson in *The Dance of Life* (1817). From a copy in the Department of Printed Books, British Museum.

*The Dance of Life* tells in rhyming couplets of semi-humorous doggerel verse, the course of a young man's life from birth to marriage. The present illustration shows how:—

> Of four-in-hand he joins the vulgar rage,
> Wields the long whip, and overturns a Stage.

The illustration may be compared with that of the XVIIIth century stage coach on the Dover Road in Volume III of this history (§ 74).

§ 40 (cf. text p. 41)

The 'Bull and Mouth' Yard. From a colour print by Henry Alken in *Real Life in London,* by an Amateur (1821). From a copy in the Department of Printed Books, British Museum.

The 'Bull and Mouth' coaching inn was on the site of the present London G.P.O. On the right of the yard lay the coach office for receiving bookings and delivering parcels and taking places for passengers; on the left, the hotel and coffee house, while the rest of the building (and most of the rest of Bull and Mouth Street) was devoted to stables, waggon and coach houses and out-offices. Here stages and mail coaches left by day and night.

§ 41 (cf. text p. 40)

The Duel. From a colour print by Robert Cruikshank in *The English Spy,* by Bernard Blackmantle (C. M. Westmacott) (1825–1826). From a copy in the Cambridge University Library.

'The practice of duelling,' says *The English Spy,* 'has become almost a profession and the privacy with which it is of necessity conducted renders it always subject to suspicion.' This scene of a duel in Hyde Park is entitled 'The Point of Honor Decided: or the Leaden Arguments of a Love Affair.'

Hyde Park was for more than two hundred years a most fashionable site for duels. Sunday was a favourite day and they usually took place in the early morning or late in the evening just near where the Serpentine lies to-day, south of what was then the Ring. (For a general note on the Cruikshanks cf. note to § 29 and 30.)

§ 42 (cf. text p. 42)

The poacher's family plead his pardon before the squire. From a coloured etching by Thomas Rowlandson in *The Dance of Life* (1817). From a copy in the Department of Printed Books, British Museum.

The same young man who has rebuilt his mansion to conform to fashionable taste (cf. § 58) and has been a rip on the roads (cf.

§ 39) has now married and at his seat at Graceful Hall administers justice. Before him Joseph Toms is brought by one of his gamekeepers, as having set a snare and caught a hare. The poacher's miserable wife and family plead his cause with Sir Harry, who persuaded by his own wife, forgives the poacher. The illustration and its accompanying text are of double interest, since besides the picture provided of a typical poaching incident, we are given a glimpse of a typical squire—on whom rested the responsibility of enforcing the severe poaching laws.

§ 43 (cf. text p. 41)

Partridge Shooting. From a colour engraving by Samuel Howett in *British Field Sports*. Published by Edward Orme (1807). From the copy in the Department of Printed Books, British Museum.

Samuel Howett (1765–1822) was Rowlandson's brother-in-law. He exhibited pictures on sporting subjects at the Royal Academy. These coloured engravings are delightfully illustrative of the English countryside and the sports appropriate to each season in its turn. For their subjects cf. text pp. 40, 41. Another example of Howett's work can be seen in Colour Plate I.

§ 44 (cf. text p. 41)

Hunters coming by surprise on a tigress. From a coloured print in *Oriental Field Sports* (1807–19). Published by Edward Orme from the MS. and designs of Captain Thomas Williamson, the drawings by Samuel Howett. From the copy in the Department of Printed Books, British Museum.

Sport was a favourite subject for the colour print and not only that in English woods and fields. Here Samuel Howett has depicted an Indian scene: a party hog-hunting has unexpectedly come upon a tigress and her cubs. The accompanying text by Captain Williamson is instructive in intent as well as descriptive: attention is called to the young man in the centre who has allowed his horse to turn, thus exposing his back to the tigress' spring. The decorative treatment of the grasses and the whole composition of the illustration are worth noting for the high degree of excellence achieved in this type of print, which (as can be seen) did not depend entirely for its charm on colour.

§ 45, 46, 47 and 48 (cf. text pp. 56, 57)

Harrow Schoolroom, Cricket at Rugby, Dormitory at Westminster, and Refectory of the King's Scholars at Westminster. From coloured plates in *History of the Colleges of Winchester, Eton*

*and Westminster*, etc. Published by Rudolph Ackermann (1816).
From a copy in the Cambridge University Library.
These four plates are given to illustrate typical public school
conditions prior to Dr. Arnold's reforms.

§ 49 (cf. text p. 57)

Thomas Arnold. From the portrait by T. Phillips (1839) in the
National Portrait Gallery.
Dr. Thomas Arnold (1795–1842) became Headmaster of Rugby
in 1828 and Professor of Modern History at Oxford in 1841.
Deeply interested in social and educational questions as well as
in religious and historical subjects, he devoted himself to giving
a new moral impulse to education on a firm basis of reformed
method.

§ 50 (cf. text p. 59)

John Stuart Mill. From the portrait by G. F. Watts (1874) in
the National Portrait Gallery.
John Stuart Mill (1806–73) was educated by his father on an
exclusively intellectual basis—the classics, history and political
economy, logic and mathematics had all formed subjects of study
before he was fourteen. A writer on, and reviewer of, literary
and philosophical themes, his political and social ideas were
advanced, in that he advocated the rights of men and women to
liberty of life and thought, with freedom from the shackles of
convention.

§ 51 (cf. text p. 59)

Thomas Carlyle. From the portrait by Sir John Millais in the
National Portrait Gallery.
Thomas Carlyle (1795–1881) began his mature life as a schoolmaster but soon took up literary work, contributing to the
*Edinburgh Review*, the *London Magazine*, *Fraser's* and other
journals. German literature, history and contemporary economic
and social conditions formed the main subjects of his writings
from the *Life of Schiller* and *The French Revolution* to such works
as *Chartism* and *Past and Present* and his lectures *On Heroes, Hero
Worship and the Heroic in History*. The political economy of the
day incurred his fiercest contempt; return to the Middle Ages
and the rule of 'the hero' constituting his gospel.

§ 52 (cf. text p. 59)

John Ruskin. From the portrait by H. von Herkomer (1881) in
the National Portrait Gallery.
John Ruskin (1819–1900) is illustrated here mainly because of

his influence on XIXth century art and architecture, though his ideas on social reform and his insistence that beauty is only compatible with truth and virtue are of interest in their context of mid-Victorian thought, especially at a time when so much stress was laid on material wealth. In *Modern Painters* he defended Turner's work and later went on to praise the Pre-Raphaelites, but in the *Seven Lamps of Architecture* and *Stones of Venice* he advocated the return to Gothic architecture (especially to Italian Gothic) (cf. § 65 described by Charles Eastlake as 'one of the firstfruits of Mr. Ruskin's teaching'—the University Museum at Oxford).

In practical illustration of his views on social subjects he founded the Guild of St. George and encouraged, for instance, revival of the hand-made linen industry in Langdale.

It is worth noting that Carlyle, Ruskin and William Morris all looked back to the mediaeval for inspiration.

§ 53 (cf. text p. 61)

'Appropriate situations for Norman, Tudor, Grecian and Roman residences.' Engraving from *Domestic Architecture*, by Richard Brown (1841). From a copy in the Department of Printed Books, British Museum.

The XIXth century passion for residences in the style of former ages is well documented by this book, which is almost a pattern book for villas and houses of all descriptions, cut to individual requirements: cottages ornées vie with examples of Elizabethan timbering, a 'Pompeian suburban villa' with an 'Egyptian Pavilion,' or villas à la grecque with those à la Florentine.

The plate reproduced here is designed to show how well they may all be adapted to suit English tastes and in which situations they may best be located; if fancy prompted a mediaeval castle, a steep bluff was the proper *mise en scène*, a classical mansion required spacious lawns and embosoming woodland, whereas a gabled manor of Tudor or Elizabethan style should lie deep in trees on the bank of a gently meandering stream.

Besides describing each individual style and its relation to the landscape, the author discusses such important topics as the layout of the grounds, the designing of garden temples and the like.

§ 54 and 56 (cf. text p. 61)

The old and new castles of Balmoral. From vignette wood engravings by J. D. Cooper, after a sketch by W. Wyld (of the old castle) and from a photograph (of the new castle) in Queen Victoria's *Leaves from the Journal of our Life in the Highlands*

(*1848–61*). Illustrated edition, edited by Arthur Helps (1868). From a copy in the Department of Printed Books, British Museum.

The old castle at Balmoral was described by the Queen in her Journal as 'A pretty little castle in the old Scottish style' (8 September 1848). Seven years later she notes 'The new house looks beautiful,' and finally on 30 August 1856 (with a note of triumph) 'The old castle gone and the tower completed.'

(Interiors of Balmoral in 1857 can be seen at § 57 and Colour Plate III).

§ 55 (cf. text p. 61)

Prince Albert at Balmoral. From a steel engraving by F. Bacon (after Landseer's painting) in Queen Victoria's *Leaves from the Journal of our Life in the Highlands* (*1848–61*). Illustrated edition, edited by Arthur Helps (1868). From a copy in the Department of Printed Books, British Museum.

In this volume published in memory of the Prince Consort this engraving of the Prince with the stag he has shot forms the frontispiece. The scene is Balmoral Forest in 1860, the Queen can be seen on horseback in the background.

§ 56 (see under note to § 54 above)

§ 57 (cf. text p. 61)

Prince Albert's study at Balmoral. From a chromolithograph after a painting by J. Roberts in Queen Victoria's *Leaves from the Journal of our Life in the Highlands* (*1848–61*). Illustrated edition, edited by Arthur Helps (1868). From a copy in the Department of Printed Books, British Museum.

This illustration of the Prince Consort's sitting room as it was in September 1857 with its simplicity—bareness almost if viewed in relation to the prevailing taste of the time—is an interesting commentary on the Prince and an excellent foil to Landseer's flamboyant and humourless picture of him (cf. § 55). Furnishing at Balmoral was planned on 'cottage' lines and the simple chintzes and absence of elaboration of detail might well have been copied with advantage in many a contemporary interior. (The companion illustration of the Queen's sitting room at Balmoral may be seen in Colour Plate III.)

§ 58 (cf. text p. 61)

'He pulls his mansion down to show his taste.' From a coloured etching by Rowlandson in The *Dance of Life* (1817). From a copy in the Department of Printed Books, British Museum.

The young squire whose prowess on the roads is pictured in

§ 39 is shown here in the clutches of 'Taste' who whispers in his ear:—

> But then the House distracts the View,
> A structure strange, half old, half new:
> The *old* is but a cumb'rous pile
> The *new* is in a wretched style;
> 'Tis my advice, the place to crown,
> Without delay to pull it down
> And build anew. . . .
>
> . . .
>
> The work of no inferior hands;
> Where use and elegance combine,
> Where Attic symmetry may join,
> To form a grand, and chaste design.
>
> . . .
>
> When lo the Architects appear,
> With anxious hope, the pile to rear:
> The masons shout, the sculptors bend,
> The artists and their arts attend:
> All preparation's duly made,
> And the first stone in pomp is laid.
> Palladio and Vitruvius groan
> Beneath the enormous weight of stone:
> The walls ascend, the columns rise;
> Taste rules the work, the money flies.
>
> *(The Dunce of Life)*

§ 59 (cf. text p. 61)

A villa in Regent's Park. From an engraving by T. H. Shepherd in James Elmes' *Metropolitan Improvements or London in the Nineteenth Century* (1827–8). From a copy in the Department of Printed Books, British Museum.

The author of this book defines the villa as 'the mere personal property and residence of the owner, where he retires to enjoy himself without state.' While making the distinction clear between the villa and the palace or mansion (as dwellings of state) he is careful to explain the difference of this type of residence from 'those merchants' and sugar-bakers' boxes which crowd the sides of Clapham Road and Kennington Common.' (Cf. the suburban villas in § 60.)

The present illustration is that of Grove House, at that time belonging to G. B. Greenough, Esq., and built by Decimus Burton; its Ionic portico is raised on a terrace and flanked by wings with Doric columns. It should be contrasted with § 61.

§ 60 (cf. text p. 61)

New Buildings, Gascoyne Road, Cassland Estate, Hackney. Architect G. Wales. From a lithograph in the possession of the Society of Antiquaries.

These mid-Victorian suburban villas are typical of many small and medium-sized houses being built all round the outskirts of London in the middle years of the century. As residential urban development they may be contrasted with industrial town development on another level in § 69. The Cassland Estate was developed about 1855 to the plans of one, George Wales, a surveyor.

§ 61 (cf. text p. 61)

A mid-Victorian clergyman's residence. Quar Wood (near Stow-on-the-Wold), Gloucestershire (1857). From *A History of the Gothic Revival*, by Charles L. Eastlake (1872). From a copy in the Department of Printed Books, British Museum.

This house, designed by J. L. Pearson in 1857, for the Rev. R. W. Hippisley, is shown as an example of one type of house being erected in the middle of the century. Its architect based his designs on the current understanding of the principles of mediaeval art (this example purports to be early XIVth century in style, exhibiting some continental influence). It should be contrasted with § 59 to assess the full difference of thought and feeling between Decimus Burton and J. L. Pearson, or, for that matter between Mr. G. B. Greenough and the Rev. R. W. Hippisley. It is perhaps only fair to add that J. L. Pearson (1817–97) left much notable work in church architecture.

§ 62 (cf. text p. 61)

Eaton Hall, Cheshire. From a drawing by J. Buckler (drawn on stone by J. D. Harding) for J. C. Buckler's *Views of Eaton Hall, Cheshire* (1826). From a copy in the Cambridge University Library.

This illustration shows the earlier Eaton Hall, begun by William Porden (a pupil of James Wyatt) in 1803, and is given as an example of 'Cathedral' Gothic as distinct from 'Castle' Gothic (displayed in the following illustration § 63).

Here the inspiration is obviously ecclesiastical and not domestic, and has given birth to towers and crenellations, pointed windows with tracery (in cast iron), fan vaulting and canopied niches. It may be remembered that Dr. Syntax in search of consolation paid a visit to Eaton Hall in 1820 and his soliloquy on that occasion throws an interesting light on one school (at least) of contemporary taste:—

I think that it should be the aim
Of families of ancient name,
Never, from fashion, to transfer
Their long established character;

. . .

The new rais'd structure should dispense
The style of old magnificence:
The grandeur of a former age
Should still the wondring eye engage,
And the last Heir be proud to raise
A mansion as of former days.

. . .

The last successor claims the praise,
For virtue in these later days,
Still as his embower'd roofs he sees,
And walls bedeck'd with traceries,
Windows with rainbow colours bright,
With many a fancied symbol dight,
And when he views the turrets rise
In bold irregularities;
He feels what no Corinthian pile
Would tell, though of the richest style,
That warriors, statesmen, learned sages,
Had borne his name in former ages,
While he, by ev'ry virtue known,
Does honour to it in his own.

(Canto XXX. *The Second Tour of Dr. Syntax
in Search of Consolation*)

§ 63 (cf. text p. 61)

Goodrich Court, Herefordshire. From an air photograph by
Aerofilms, Ltd.

Built (between 1828 and 1831) by Edward Blore (1787–1879)
for Sir Samuel Meyrick, to house the latter's great collection of
armour, this sham castle is of particular interest in that besides
providing an example of a neo-Gothic interpretation of a
mediaeval castle, its prototype can be seen across the valley.
This should not be interpreted to mean that the Court was a
slavish copy of the Castle—far from it, but some of the characteristic features of Goodrich and other castles of the Marches
(notably for instance the triangular buttressing of the great
corner towers) were reproduced by Blore at Goodrich Court:
the Court was demolished in 1950.

Blore was architect, topographical artist and antiquary. He

supplied the inspiration for Abbotsford for Sir Walter Scott, was concerned in reconstruction work at Buckingham Palace and was also surveyor to Westminster Abbey. His work as topographer has been illustrated in several examples in earlier volumes of this history (e.g. Vol. I, § 96, 127, 149, 156, 162; Vol. II, § 10, 11), while his antiquarian interests (besides being apparent in his architectural work) are evidenced by his *Monumental Remains of Eminent Persons* (1824) and the work he did for Scott on the *Provincial Antiquities of Scotland* as well as in his illustrations for his father's *History of Rutland* and Surtees' *Antiquities of Durham*.

Blore's reputation in the neo-Gothic movement is indicated by Thomas Dibdin in his *Northern Tour* (1838), where he refers to Lord Corehouse's 'beautiful Gothic Villa' built 'under the unerring guidance of Mr. Blore.'

§ 64 (cf. text p. 17)

London University. From an engraving in T. H. Shepherd's *The World's Metropolis* (1857). From a copy in the Cambridge University Library.

London University (founded 1827) was designed by William Wilkins, R.A.; and built under the direction of J. Gandy Deering, A.R.A. The building illustrated here is, of course, that now known as University College, Gower Street. It should be contrasted in style with a University building in the next illustration (§ 65). London in 1827 drew its inspiration for a new University from classic style, Oxford in 1855 for its new science museum embraced the neo-Gothic (cf. note below to § 65).

§ 65 (cf. text p. 62)

The University Museum, Oxford. From *A History of the Gothic Revival*, by Charles L. Eastlake (1872). From a copy in the Department of Printed Books, British Museum.

This illustration of a University building begun in 1855 should be contrasted with the foregoing one of London University (1827), in order to realize the difference that divides the two—a difference already instanced and paralleled between § 59 and 61. This building—the Museum of Physical Sciences—is called by Charles Eastlake 'one of the firstfruits of Mr. Ruskin's teaching'; carried out by Messrs. Deane and Woodward, it is an example of the deliberately introduced Italian Gothic, sponsored by Ruskin, though there are other influences as well: Eastlake points out the laboratory on the right of the main front as reminiscent of the Abbot's Kitchen at Glastonbury—as indeed it is in general outline at least.

In the interior the architects endeavoured to realize the principles of *The Seven Lamps of Architecture*, that is, not by mere reproduction of mediaeval decorative features but by trying to imbue their work with the mediaeval spirit, translating it into terms of modern materials, such as cast iron.

§ 66 (cf. text p. 59)

Charles Dickens. From the portrait by A. Scheffer (1855) in the National Portrait Gallery.

This and the following portrait of Thackeray are given to illustrate the essentially XIXth century development of the novel, and particularly that of the novel of social satire. In a host of novels Dickens sought to bring home to the public of his day the evils of the slums or the need for prison reform. Against a teeming background of every type of character and class, rich in humour and eccentricity, he held up to ridicule or censure, the hypocrite and the miser, the 'Philistine' and the shabby genteel, the new rich, the church, the aristocracy, the industrialist, but in so doing extracted the maximum amount of pathos on behalf of the oppressed and helpless.

§ 67 (cf. text p. 59)

W. M. Thackeray. From the oil sketch by Samuel Laurence in the National Portrait Gallery.

Thackeray on the other hand (cf. with note above on Charles Dickens) used his satirical pen to extract the maximum entertainment from social pretentiousness, and to draw in broad lines the passing life of his age (as Fielding and Smollett had done before him). He did not confine himself however to tilting at nabobs and adventuresses, or contrasting simple characters, such as Colonel Newcome, with the world in which they found themselves, but turned to the previous century to give a vivid period piece in *Henry Esmond*.

§ 68 (cf. text p. 65)

A Yorkshire woollen mill. From an air photograph by Aerofilms, Ltd., by courtesy of Messrs. James Ives & Co., Ltd., Yeadon, Leeds.

This illustration is shown as a typical example of the way in which industrial growth in the XIXth and XXth centuries has gradually changed the face of agricultural country. It should be compared with earlier examples in XVIIIth century England (e.g. cf. the illustrations of a cotton twist mill and a copper and brassworks of the 1780's in Volume III of this history—§ 64 and 65) where the immediate surroundings are still completely rural. Here the original mill buildings (dating from 1862) can be seen in the centre of the group of mill buildings—the tall pedimented block on the right and the low block on the left. Around them have gradually grown up more buildings as and when they were needed for expansion or new developments in production. In the foreground can be seen the older cottages in which the workers would be housed, as yet irregularly set like any village layout, on the left further in the distance can be seen later terrace houses, approximating more closely to the typical XIXth century industrial town development (to be seen at its most mass-produced in the following illustration § 69) and to the right and in the general background newer building development, where spacing and garden allotment mark a change in outlook from the last century's overcrowded industrial housing schemes.

§ 69 (cf. text pp. 62, 118)

Industrial housing at Burnley, Lancashire. From an air photograph by Aerofilms, Ltd.

This air photograph is given to illustrate the enormous change that the industrial XIXth century made in town development. The maximum number of small houses was designed to fill the given space, each exactly like its neighbours, each street the counterpart of the adjoining ones. The factory chimneys can be seen on the left, right in the middle of the 'back-to-backs' themselves.

This example of what happened in actuality should be contrasted with Robert Owen's dream of small industrial communities living with dignity amid open surroundings (cf. § 22).

§70, 71, 72, 73 and 74 (cf. text pp. 61, 63)

From woodcuts in the *Foreign Tour of Brown, Jones and Robinson*, by Richard Doyle (1854).

Richard Doyle (1824–1883), son of 'H. B.' (the political caricaturist), is a great way in spirit from earlier caricaturists such as Gillray and Rowlandson, as indeed he is from his contemporary John Leech, a fellow contributor to *Punch*. 'Dicky' Doyle joined the staff of *Punch* in 1843 and in 1849 designed the cover which it has retained ever since. In the same year *Punch* contained the first sketches of what were afterwards to become *Manners and Customs of Ye Englyshe*. (These delightful commentaries on the contemporary social scene are exemplified in textual illustrations on pp. 54, 62, 69 and 76 in the present volume.) Doyle left *Punch* in 1850 (due to differences on the paper's anti-papal policy) and devoted himself to book-illustration. Four years later appeared the delicious *Foreign Tour* from which § 70 to 74 are taken. Doyle pokes gentle fun at the insularity and self-sufficiency of the 'Great Briton' and the English 'milord' on the Rhine, and shows his naive trio at the Academy in Venice sampling Art, or on the outside seats of a diligence on the St. Gothard 'the better to enjoy the grandeur of the scenery'. The delicacy of line in these woodblocks, the knack of crowd work, the quiet fun are inimitable. Note for instance how 'milord' immerses himself in the *Quarterly* and *The Times*, look at the copyists and guide lecturers in the Academy, and the conscious air of doing the thing properly on the Grand Canal.

§ 75 (cf. text p. 66)

A Court for King Cholera. From John Leech's *Later Pencillings from Punch* (1864). From a copy in the Cambridge University Library.

John Leech (1817–1864), caricaturist and contributor to *Punch* and author of sporting sketches, is master of a harsher tone and more incisive wit than gentle 'Dicky' Doyle. His Rick Burner's Home (§ 90) on the one hand, and his Enquiry into the Income of Bishops (textual illustration on p. 46) or even his Navvy (textual illustration p. 87) or Road Sweeper (textual illustration p. 73) form an interesting contrast to Doyle's reaction to the contemporary scene (for note on Doyle cf. note to § 70–74 above), but even at his harshest Leech is genial compared with Gillray as a caricaturist. Apart from his woodcuts for Surtees' *Handley Cross* and *Mr. Sponge*, Leech poured out cartoons and sketches for *Punch* from 1840 onwards, which unfold a commentary on dress and manners, contemporary politics, reforms and abuses, and topical matters of all kinds for the middle years of the Century.

This scene at the back of Oxford Street as late as the sixties is a horrid reminder of slum conditions in the capital and elsewhere at this date. It is typical of the area known as 'The Rookery', which stretched from Great Russell Street to St. Giles's, with its open midden, its foul overcrowded tenements and filthy ragged denizens.

§ 76 (cf. text p. 67)

Going to the Great Exhibition. From Henry Mayhew's *1851 or the Adventures of Mr. and Mrs. Sandboys and family*. Illustrated by H. M. and G. Cruikshank. From a copy in the Cambridge University Library.

Mayhew and Cruikshank managed to extract plenty of fun from

the visit of the provincials to the Great Exhibition, and not by any means at the expense of the provincials only. This illustration shows the transport problem and incidentally gives a good close-up of the horse-bus of the period (other examples of buses of this period and later in the century may be seen at § 78 and 79 and 129 and 133 below and Colour Plate IV; cf. note to the last for a general note on buses). (For a general note on the Cruikshanks cf. note to § 29 and 30.)

§ 77 (cf. text p. 67)

The Great Exhibition. 'Taken on the spot' by George Cruikshank and published by Daniel Bogue (on 28 June 1851). This shows the opening of the Great Exhibition on 1 May 1851. The Queen and the Prince Consort with the rest of the Royal party can be seen on the dais under the canopy; the Archbishop of Canterbury is offering up a prayer 'for the Divine Blessing upon the objects of this Great Exhibition.' In the right foreground can be seen Osler's Crystal Fountain. (For a general note on the Cruikshanks cf. note to § 29 and § 30.)

§ 78 (cf. text p. 70)

Hyde Park in 1842. From *Original Views of London as it really is*, by Thomas Shotter Boys (with notes by Charles Ollier) (1842). From a copy in the Department of Printed Books, British Museum.

This lithograph shows Hyde Park (near Grosvenor Gate) with a fashionable crowd on horseback, in carriages or on foot. The view is taken looking up what is now Park Lane towards Marble Arch. Ollier in his notes contrasts the 'indolent ease,' the aristocratic loungers, with the busy city scenes, which Shotter Boys illustrates in the same volume. He points out Tyburn (in the extreme distance) as 'the spot where repose the ashes of the stern usurper Oliver Cromwell'; the building on the right (with columns) as the Library built as a picture gallery for the Marquis of Westminster's mansion to house his collection of Rubens' paintings. On the left in the middle distance he calls attention to 'the pretty Grecian building' for a lodge for the keeper of Grosvenor Gate, and in the furthest distance the roofs of Hyde Park Place—the western terminus of Oxford Street. This illustration of a fashionable promenade in the middle XIXth century might be compared with the Mall in 1735 (Volume III, § 7) and with Du Maurier's drawing in 1885 of the 'Row' (§ 117 in this volume).

§ 79 and 80 (cf. text p. 70)

Marble Arch and Regent Street. From engravings in *The World's Metropolis*, by T. H. Shepherd (1857). From a copy in the Cambridge University Library.

§ 79 shows Marble Arch in 1857, with a horse-bus, carriage and riders. Marble Arch had been built as an entry to Buckingham Palace in 1828 and was not erected in its present position until 1851 (where it is shown in this illustration). As can be seen from this it was at this time an actual entrance to the Park itself, it was only after changes early in the XXth century that it was islanded in the middle of the roadway.

§ 80 shows Nash's Regent Street (since destroyed and super seded) with its elegant curve, built between 1813 and 1820 to connect Carlton House with the Regent's Park. A greater contrast between the traffic illustrated here (both in type and concentration) and that of to-day at this same spot can hardly be imagined. Note the typical regency balconies and the decoration of the colonnade on the left.
The bus is plying between Chelsea and Islington. Note the Provident Life Office (County Fire Office) almost the only familiar point to our eyes.

§ 81 (cf. text p. 70)

The river by Lambeth Palace. From an engraving in *The World's Metropolis*, by T. H. Shepherd (1857). From a copy in the Cambridge University Library.
The river was still used as a highway to a greater extent in the middle of the XIXth century than it is to-day. This busy scene by Lambeth Palace shows boats of all kinds including a paddle steamer in the foreground. Lambeth Bridge, which followed the line of the ferry between Millbank and Lambeth Palace, was not yet built; this ferry can be seen on the right.

§ 82 and 83 (cf. text p. 85)

Two details from Frith's 'Derby Day' (1858) in the Tate Gallery, London. (By courtesy of the Trustees.)
A cross-section of mid-Victorian types and classes is afforded us in Frith's 'Derby Day': the course, the side-shows, the child performers, the gypsies, the carriage parties—all are included with photographic clarity and detail. Frith's diary tells us that the first sketches for this were made in May 1856, individual figure studies were also made and a small oil sketch of the overall scene led to his being commissioned to paint this subject in full. Work on this was begun in January 1857 and it was

finished in time for the Academy Exhibition of 1858; though certain alterations were made in it after exhibition. Several of the figures were painted from Frith's family or friends.

These two contrasted details are given to show the varied crowd, the mixture of types and classes, the minutiae of dress and style. Though the scene is somewhat consciously posed and idealized, as with nearly all Frith's work, it is a fair sample of Victorian anecdotal painting. (Cf. § 37 and 38 for Regency racing scenes.)

§ 84 (cf. text p. 89)

Eastward Ho! August 1857. From the original painting by Henry N. O'Neil in the possession of Major Sir Richard G. Proby.

The Indian Mutiny and the war in China gave occasion for many such scenes as these in the fifties; the troopship is about to sail and wives and families are coming on shore after leave-taking. 1857 had seen the massacre at Cawnpore and the siege of Delhi, the Relief of Lucknow was to come that September.

This was one of the most popular of O'Neil's paintings. Born in 1817 in St. Petersburg, O'Neil exhibited at the Academy from 1838–79. He painted historical and genre subjects as well as landscape and died in 1880.

§ 85 (cf. text p. 68)

From the original water-colour sketch by John Dobbin of the opening of the Stockton and Darlington Railway in September 1825, in the Science Museum, South Kensington. (By courtesy of the Director of the Science Museum.)

This amateur sketch of the opening in 1825 of the first passenger railway line in England is engaging as a curiosity, even if it cannot be claimed that the engine for instance is an accurate representation.

The immediate forerunner of the railway proper had been the system of wooden rails and planks (later replaced by iron plates) over which horses drew waggons of coal (an example can be seen in § 17 where the gradient served instead of horse power) and the type of waggon is much the same as Grimm had sketched at the end of the XVIIIth century near Newcastle (cf. Volume III, § 63). An early steam engine with trucks can be seen in § 15 in use at a Yorkshire colliery. The first user of steam traction was Richard Trevithick in South Wales in 1804 but the passenger train did not occur until 1825 on the Stockton and Darlington Railway illustrated here: George Stephenson was

the engineer employed. The final success of the steam locomotive was established some five years later with the building
of the Liverpool and Manchester Railway (cf. § 21, which shows
the building of the embankment and tunnel at Edge Hill on this
line in 1830). A full description of the opening of the Stockton
and Darlington line is given in Longridge's account of it published in 1827 at Newcastle. The locomotive was driven by
George Stephenson, followed by a tender with coals and water,
together with more waggons loaded with the same, a covered
coach with the Committee and railway proprietors, and finally
twenty-one waggons for passengers. This sketch shows the
covered coach, the passengers and the engine but no coal
waggons. (For other railway scenes cf. also § 86–89, and textual
illustration p. 69).

§ 86 and 87 (cf. text pp. 68, 69)

'Building a retaining wall at Camden Town' and 'Entrance to
the Locomotive Engine House, Camden Town.' From John C.
Bourne's *Drawings of the London and Birmingham Railway* (1839),
text by John Britton. From a copy in the Cambridge University
Library.
The London and Birmingham Railway was the first main line
from London, it was amalgamated with the Liverpool and
Manchester Railway (cf. § 21) and the Grand Junction and
Manchester and Birmingham lines in 1846 to form the London
and North-Western Railway.
These two illustrations show the building of the retaining wall
(17 September 1838)—which operation was described by
Dickens in *Dombey and Son*—and the entrance to the locomotive
sheds at the same place, with a typical engine of the time.
The first engine to be used commercially was Blenkinsop's (cf.
§ 15), to be followed by 'Puffing Billy' (1813), the Stockton and
Darlington locomotive (1825) (cf. § 85) and the 'Rocket' (1829).
All these were built on the same general principle and do not
differ in basic form from the engines illustrated in § 87, though
the design is becoming more 'tailored.'

§ 88 and 89 (cf. text pp. 68, 69)

Pangbourne Station and Bristol Station. From John C. Bourne's
*History and Description of the Great Western Railway* (1846). From
a copy in the Cambridge University Library.
These two engravings are contrasted to show a small country
station and an important city station. Examples of the first can
be seen still with very little alteration up and down England to-
day, its style will be familiar to all. In the plate of Bristol station,

particular interest centres on the 'Gothic' structure of the building, its strong ecclesiastical flavour;—arches, columns, capitals and hammer-beam roof—functional architecture is still far in the future. § 89 shows a broad gauge locomotive, carriages and trucks.

§ 90, 91 and 92 (cf. text pp. 75, 77, 86)

'The Home of the Rick Burner' (1844), 'Peel's Cheap Bread Shop' (1846) and 'Emigration a Remedy' (1848). From cartoons by John Leech in *Early Pencillings from Punch* (1864). From a copy in the Cambridge University Library.

These drawings by Leech tell their own tale of agricultural distress, of economic difficulties and of attempts to alleviate the lot of some at least by emigration, with a culminating scene conjuring up colonial wealth and plenty.

The protective Corn Law of 1815 which had benefited the farmer at the expense of the consumer (cf. text p. 3) was repealed in 1846, making cheap bread for the populace the objective rather than the protected prosperity of the farmer against foreign competition. (For satirical comment on the farmer's position cf. textual illustration p. 76). The agricultural labourer's plight was brought about partly by the new Poor Law depriving him of outdoor relief, partly by the threat of unemployment and lower wages, due to the introduction of machinery—cheap bread was therefore the only thing to keep him from starving. Landowners and farmers on the other hand wanted corn prices kept high (and cheap foreign corn kept out) to ensure profits and rents. Peel was intent on making England a cheap country for living and therefore first lowered and then removed import duties on most raw materials. The repeal of the Corn Laws followed in June 1846. Note the drawing of the emigration scene shows placards on the wall against vagrants and Chartists—'all such meetings illegal'. (For a general note on Leech cf. note to § 75.)

§ 93 and 94 (cf. text p. 81)

Child labour in the textile factories. From illustrations in *Life and Adventures of Michael Armstrong the Factory Boy*, by Frances Trollope (1840). From a copy in the Department of Printed Books, British Museum.

Frances Trollope fresh from her onslaughts on life in the United States (1832) turned her attention at home to the horrors and abuses of the employment of child labour in the textile factories. In her story of a child apprentice, she claims that her description of Deep Valley Mill is that of a real mill in Derbyshire, and based on unimpeachable authority (footnote to p. 149 of Vol. II of the *Life*).

§ 93 shows the interior of a mill—the well-dressed visitors, who have just called, contrast with the ragged apprentices and slatternly workers. Michael who has been put to work at the 'mules' to repair breakings of the threads, is greeting one of his former playmates.

§ 94 shows ragged half-starved factory children scrambling for food at the pig-trough in the farmyard adjoining the factory. The text describes how the fare provided was miserable water porridge and lumps of oaten cake; the pig-trough represented the 'tit-bits'—'dainty eating for the starving prentices of Deep Valley Mill.' They slept on bundles of straw and the rule was that the children should work overtime to ensure that no valuable customer was disappointed. These conditions should be contrasted with the note to § 64 in Vol. III of this history to see how far conditions had worsened in a bare forty-five years.

§ 95 (cf. text p. 81)
Anti-Slavery Society Convention (1840). From the original painting by B. R. Haydon in the National Portrait Gallery.
This Convention was held at the Freemasons' Hall, London, in June 1840. The President, Thomas Clarkson, is addressing the meeting. It is reproduced here, partly to show the interest in England for the abolition of slavery, but also by way of commentary on the conscience which could condone industrial conditions at home (as they existed even after the 1833 Factory Act), while deploring another country's employment of slave labour.

§ 96 and 97 (cf. text p. 88)
Scenes in the Crimea. From illustrations (from sketches made on the spot by W. Simpson) in George Brackenbury's *Campaign in the Crimea* (1855–6). From a copy in the Cambridge University Library.
These illustrations show the conditions that ill-equipped troops had to face throughout the winter after Balaclava, and (in § 97) a hospital ward at Scutari, under Florence Nightingale's rule. The Crimean was the first war in which war correspondents (representing the daily papers) accompanied the army and sent back despatches. William Simpson (1823–99) acted as war artist with the British Army, making drawings which were later published by Colnaghi and Sons as 'Illustrations of the War in

the East' (1855–6). Simpson afterwards joined the staff of the *Illustrated London News* and served as artist in many subsequent theatres of war.

(For a typical 'navvy' sent out to build roads in the Crimea cf. textual illustration on p. 87).

§ 98 (cf. text p. 60 and 106 note).

Alfred Tennyson. From the portrait by G. F. Watts (1873) in the National Portrait Gallery.

Alfred Tennyson (1809–92) who in 1850 succeeded Wordsworth as Poet Laureate, in his hovering between faith and doubt in *In Memoriam* and in his romantic treatment of King Arthur and his knights in *Idylls of the King* is typical of his age. The high finish of his verse, with its polished imagery and the virtuosity of its vowel music, is the exact counterpart of the high technical finish of contemporary painting, the subjects often akin in popular sentimental appeal.

§ 99 (cf. text p. 109).

William Morris. From the portrait by G. F. Watts (1880) in the National Portrait Gallery.

William Morris (1834–96) is selected here as a man who stood head and shoulders above his age, and who, possessed of demoniac energy of mind and body, was painter and poet, designer and maker of furniture and textiles, printer and producer of fine books and, finally, social reformer. He revolutionized taste in the latter part of the century and Morris hangings and wallpapers became the hall-mark of the 'new look' in interior decoration. His Kelmscott Press (established 1890) turned out elaborate editions based on Morris-designed founts and Morris ornamental borders, while in the middle of the century he had helped to paint the frescoes at the Oxford Union. In poetry and prose he ranged from the *Earthly Paradise* and *Sigurd the Volsung* to *News from Nowhere* and *The Dream of John Ball*; the influences of the mediaeval romance and the Scandinavian saga are strong in his verse, while his interest in socialism (based on pseudo-mediaeval ideas) influenced his prose work. It is worth remembering that he was responsible for founding the Society for the Protection of Ancient Buildings.

§100 (cf. text pp. 44 and 104)

W. E. Gladstone. From the portrait by G. F. Watts (1858) in the National Portrait Gallery.

W. E. Gladstone (1809–98) is illustrated here not only as the great Liberal statesman of his age but also as a man of his time in the high seriousness of thought and ideals, reflected faithfully in his personal life.

§ 101 (cf. text p. 106)

Charles Darwin. From the portrait by J. Collier in the National Portrait Gallery.

Charles Darwin (1809–82) by his *On the Origin of Species by Means of Natural Selection* in 1859 plunged his contemporaries into a battle of science *versus* religion that lasted for the rest of the century. The impact of unshackled enquiry on fundamentalist beliefs was necessarily noisy and far reaching in its effect.

§ 102 (cf. text p. 99)

'A Gallant Reply' (1882), by George du Maurier. From *Society Pictures from Punch* (1891). From a copy in the Department of Printed Books, British Museum.

Formality and material abundance and elegance on social occasions were still strongly evident in the eighties—for the informal background cf. § 103.

George du Maurier (1834–96) besides his work as a black and white artist published three novels. Educated in Paris he returned to London to take up a scientific career at his father's wish, though his own instincts turned to drawing and music. In 1856, on his father's death, he returned to Paris as an art student, but after four years came back to London and thereafter contributed to *Punch* and *Once a Week* and was thus launched on his career of social pictorial satire. He succeeded John Leech on the staff of *Punch* in 1864 and was a close friend of Charles Keene, whose work he much admired. Du Maurier's illustrations fall into well-defined classes and the subjects occur again and again with modifications and variations: the nouveaux riches, the aesthetes, the 'things one would rather have said differently' and so on. As a commentary on the London social scene of roughly the last thirty years of the century—their fashions and manners—they are unrivalled. In them we can trace the lavish scale of entertainment, the formality of dress and manners, or again the conscious informality of Bohemianism; large families and armies of servants, the latest craze, the beginnings of women's emancipation, tennis parties, picnics, sport, clubs, the Park—they are all here in rich profusion, though as the century wears on, the drawings become more mechanical and conventional, both in line and spirit. The charm of the early illustrations to Mrs. Gaskell's *Wives and Daughters* (1866) could not be repeated indefinitely. (Cf. § 104.)

§ 103 (cf. text p. 99)

'Late for Dinner' (1886), by George du Maurier. From *Society Pictures from Punch* (1891). From a copy in the Department of Printed Books, British Museum.

The joys of a dinner party for the younger members of the family are chronicled here (cf. the dinner party itself in § 102 above). An eager gathering on the stairs awaits the end of each course, the dishes being fallen upon as they re-appear. Note the large family of children, and the pinafores worn by the girls. (For a general note on du Maurier cf. note to § 102 above.)

§ 104 (cf. text p. 99)

Conversation Piece in 1866. Illustration by George du Maurier to *Wives and Daughters* (1866), by Mrs. Gaskell. From a copy in the Department of Printed Books, British Museum.

This typical middle class interior of the sixties should be contrasted with the much more elaborate and formal town house interior of the eighties in § 106 and with the informal country house interior of § 107. The dress is also worth comparing with that in § 105 for instance. Note the overmantel hangings, the profusion of ornaments on the mantelpiece and contrast with text illustrations on pp. 98, 99. (For a general note on du Maurier cf. note to § 102 above.)

§ 105 (cf. text p. 99)

'The Veto' (1878) by George du Maurier. From *English Society at Home* (1880). From a copy in the Department of Printed Books, British Museum.

The elaboration of dress is satirized here, as having reached the point where appearance is everything, comfort and convenience itself being entirely sacrificed to the latest craze. (For a general note on du Maurier cf. note to § 102.)

§ 106 (cf. text p. 99)

A formal interior (1878) by George du Maurier. From *English Society at Home* (1880). From a copy in the Department of Printed Books, British Museum.

This formal music room with its profusion of palms, screens and lights should be contrasted with the simple interior in § 104 or with § 107, where an informal interior, though of equal sophistication, is shown. (For a general note on du Maurier cf. note to § 102.)

§ 107 (cf. text p. 99)

'A cup of tea and a quiet cigarette after lunch" by George du Maurier. From *English Society* (1897) (reprinted from *Harper's Magazine*). A confused medley of children, dogs, billiards, music and conversation reigns here and forms an amusing contrast to the scene in § 106 with its chilly formality. (For a general note on du Maurier cf. note to § 102.)

§ 108 (cf. text p. 100)

'Amenities of the Tennis Lawn' (1883), by George du Maurier. From *Society Pictures from Punch* (1891). From a copy in the Department of Printed Books, British Museum.

Men's tennis fashions in 1883 for mixed doubles look almost as strange as the women's to modern eyes. (For a general note on du Maurier cf. note to § 102.)

§ 109 (cf. text p. 100)

'A Victorian Picnic' (1887), by George du Maurier. From *Society Pictures from Punch* (1891). From a copy in the Department of Printed Books, British Museum.

Even picnics gave little amelioration to the formality of women's dress, though men had a much easier formula. (For a general note on du Maurier cf. note to § 102.)

§ 110 (cf. text p. 100)

'Amenities of the Gentle Craft' (1885), by George du Maurier. From *Society Pictures from Punch* (1891). From a copy in the Department of Printed Books, British Museum.

Besides the realms of tennis and cycling (cf. § 108 and 127) women were also entering such sacred male preserves as fishing. Here a young woman is being initiated into the intricacies of the 'gentle craft.' (For a general note on du Maurier cf. note to § 102.)

§ 111 (cf. text p. 100)

'Clubwomen of 1878,' by George du Maurier. From *Society Pictures from Punch* (1891). From a copy in the Department of Printed Books, British Museum.

This is an amusing skit by du Maurier on female emancipation in the form of a parody on the activities and manners of club men. Women's clubs were becoming established in the eighties. (For a general note on du Maurier cf. note to § 102.)

§ 112 (cf. text p. 103)

'A London Fog.' From the drawing by W. Small, *Graphic Portfolio* (1876). From a copy in the Department of Printed Books, British Museum.

The *Graphic* specialized in social pictures and this illustration of a London fog from its portfolio published in 1876 shows some of the concomitants of a 'pea-souper'—the flares, the lost umbrellas, the pickpockets, the general confusion.

§ 113 (cf. text p. 100)

'Ramsgate Sands.' From the original painting by Arthur Boyd Houghton (1861) in the Tate Gallery, London.

This picture of Ramsgate Sands in 1861 shows children playing on the sands, while their elders sit reading on the breakwater or join in their play.

Boyd Houghton (1836–75) was both painter and book illustrator. The virtues of this painting of the life of the seaside can be emphasized by comparison with the more artificial and 'posed' piece of the same name by Frith. (Cf. also with § 114, 115 and 116).

§ 114 (cf. text p. 100)

'Pegwell Bay, Kent. A Recollection of October 5th, 1858,' by William Dyce. From the original painting in the Tate Gallery, London. (By courtesy of the Trustees.)

In this quiet seascape of attractive muted tones are one of the painter's sons, his wife and her two sisters. They illustrate a different kind of taste in holidays from that shown in § 113—seclusion and the pleasures of seeking for rare kinds of seaweed and shells (so beloved of Victorian families) take the place of the gregarious bathing and sand-castle making of Ramsgate Sands.

William Dyce (1806–64) was one of the Pre-Raphaelite group of painters and Professor of Fine Arts at King's College, London, as well as a leader in the High-Church movement. His work covered fresco and glass painting, portraiture and historical painting.

§ 115 (cf. text p. 100)

A seaside resort in the 90's. From a photograph by Mr. Tom Bright. Reproduced by courtesy of Mr. H. A. Mills through Aerofilms, Ltd.

This photograph is of twofold interest, first for its intimate picture of an unconscious seaside scene, and secondly for its own sake as a photograph of some technical achievement—note the foam pattern in the foreground, for instance.

The chief differences from to-day that strike us are the fact that everyone paddles rather than swims, that the general note in dress is dark coloured and 'stuffy,' and that the whole scene seems to us extraordinarily 'over-dressed,' used as we are to seeing the majority of people on the sands in swim-suits or light, brief clothing. (For a fashionable promenade of the same date cf. § 116 below.)

§ 116 (cf. text p. 100)

Scarborough (1899). From the *Illustrated London News* of 12 August 1899.

This scene of a fashionable promenade should be contrasted with § 115 of an informal scene on the beach of roughly the same date.

§ 117 (cf. text p. 102)

'The Park' (1885), by George du Maurier. From *Society Pictures from Punch* (1891). From a copy in the department of Printed Books, British Museum.

This scene might be contrasted with § 78 of Hyde Park in 1842. The leisurely, fashionable parade is much the same in general atmosphere, in spite of forty years' interval. (For a general note on du Maurier cf. note to § 102.)

§ 118 (cf. text p. 102)

'The Eton and Harrow Match' (1878), by George du Maurier. From *English Society at Home* (1880). From a copy in the Department of Printed Books, British Museum.

A luncheon party at Lord's provides an excellent opportunity for du Maurier to portray contemporary dress and atmosphere. (For a general note on du Maurier cf. note to § 102.)

§ 119 (cf. text p. 102)

'Humility in splendour' (1878), by George du Maurier. From *English Society at Home* (1880). From a copy in the Department of Printed Books, British Museum.

The nouveau riche in his exaggerated and grandiloquent splendour is burlesqued by du Maurier as 'finding no place like 'ome.' (For a general note on du Maurier cf. note to § 102.)

§ 120 (cf. text p. 102)

'Aesthetic with a vengeance' (1873), by George du Maurier. From *Society Pictures from Punch* (1891). From a copy in the Department of Printed Books, British Museum.

The significance of buhl and marqueterie is well understood by the two young men by the mantelpiece, even the choice of a wife is determined by her ability to 'tone' with the fashionable scheme of decoration. (For a general note on du Maurier cf. note to 102.)

§ 121 and 122 (cf. text p. 103)

'The Main Chance' (1878) and 'The Festive Season' (1883), by George du Maurier. From *Society Pictures from Punch* (1891). From a copy in the Department of Printed Books, British Museum.

Long families, especially of girls, made the question of early and advantageous marriages for their offspring a main preoccupation for Victorian parents.

Each house of any pretension had a full complement of servants, each performing the duties proper to his or her place in the hierarchy, butler and housekeeper, lady's maid and valet, parlourmaids, footmen, housemaids and kitchenmaids, and perhaps most important and demanding of all—the cook. This illustration should be compared with the two of servants (at § 18 and 19) by Rowlandson at the beginning of the century. (For a general note on du Maurier cf. note to § 102.)

§ 123 (cf. text p. 120)

'A young ladies' seminary' (1876), by George du Maurier. From *Society Pictures from Punch* (1891). From a copy in the Department of Printed Books, British Museum.

This illustration of the 'crocodile' from a young ladies' seminary might be contrasted with the illustration following of an arithmetic class under the conditions of 'free' education of some sixteen years later. (For a note on educational development cf. note to § 124.) (For a general note on du Maurier cf. note to § 102).

§ 124 (cf. text pp. 119, 120)

Free Education. Sketch from the *Illustrated London News* of 3 October 1891.

Various aspects of school life, earlier in the XIXth century have been illustrated (cf. § 45–48). Education as understood by the old free grammar schools had long passed away, private schools and academies flourished in both the XVIIIth and XIXth centuries and charity schools had been maintained since Queen Anne's reign. Successive Acts were passed which enlarged and developed the grammar school curriculum, and at the same time efforts were made to provide elementary education under a system of state grants, on a national scale—finally achieved by the 1902 Act. A special feature of the 1891 programme was free education, the Chancellor of the Exchequer producing a surplus of £2 million in his Budget—that is, roughly the sum estimated to cover the cost of remitting school fees. Elementary education became free from the 1 September of that same year.

§ 125 (cf. text pp. 90, 111)

'The Joys of Photography' (1886), by George du Maurier. From *Society Pictures from Punch* (1891). From a copy in the Department of Printed Books, British Museum.

Photography proper (preceded by the daguerrotype) is associated with the name of Fox Talbot, who in 1835 discovered how to fix his prints from sensitized paper and devised the printing of positives from negatives. This illustration shows one of du Maurier's 'gentle bearded intellectuals' (cf. p. 90) enduring the agonies of being posed for the camera. (For a general note on du Maurier cf. note to § 102.)

§ 126 (cf. text p. 113)

'Speaking to Paris from London'—completion of the Anglo-French telephone. Sketch from the *Illustrated London News* 28 March 1891.

The precursor of the telephone, which could reproduce musical sounds, was produced in 1860 by J. P. Reis, but the transmission of speech was not achieved until 1876 by Graham Bell. Communication by means of signals between London and Paris had been achieved by submarine cable in 1852 but the telephone first made it possible to communicate by direct speech from London to Paris or *vice versa*.

§ 127 (cf. text p. 100)

American Cyclists in England. Sketch from the *Illustrated London News* 9 July 1898.

The bicycle had become fashionable soon after it left the bone-shaker stage and came with rubber tyres and two wheels of the same size closer to the modern bicycle as we know it.

This illustration is of twofold interest in that it shows the extent to which the bicycle was by this time an easy, pleasant medium of getting about, but also is witness to the enthusiasm and energy of the American tourist in exploring England.

§ 128 (cf. text p. 124)

'A Steep run to Tunbridge,' Sketch from the *Illustrated London News* 16 April 1898 (Supplement).

Early self-propelled vehicles, such as Richard Trevithick's steam carriage of 1802, were the progenitors of such vehicles as the steam-buses shown in § 129. Daimler had evolved the petrol gas motor by 1884 and thereafter the internal combustion engine determined the main line of development. This illustration shows part of an Easter Motoring Meeting—the Holiday Tour of the Automobile Club.

§ 129 (cf. text p. 124)

Horse-buses racing steam-bus. Sketch from the *Illustrated London News* 18 June 1898.

Until 1896 regulations were in force to prevent mechanically propelled carriages travelling at a greater speed than four miles per hour, the propulsion of such carriages by steam or gas demanded revision of these laws and a special excursion was made from London to Brighton on 14 November of that year to celebrate the removal of the restrictions. This sketch shows the rivalry of horse-power and steam-power: the Self Acting Steam Omnibus Co. operated from Oxford Street to Ealing.

§ 130 (cf. text p. 123)

'Naval Manoeuvres—Steam Tactics.' Sketch from the *Illustrated London News* 12 August 1893.

The first use of steam for navigation dated from 1802 and in 1838 the first steamship proper crossed the Atlantic. Soon warships followed the example of the merchant navy, the use of engines for propulsion required protection against guns and demanded armour plating; the ironclads therefore came to supersede the old wooden battleships of the Victory type. Here one can see the heavy armament and modification of design that have accompanied the change over and subsequent development of the fleet.

§ 131 and 132 (cf. text p. 109)

'The nineties.' From photographs of 1899 by Mr. Tom Bright. Reproduced by courtesy of Mr. H. A. Mills through Aerofilms, Ltd.

The first photograph, § 131, showing poster hoardings by the Old Alhambra in Leicester Square, includes many advertisements that are still household names to-day; it is reproduced here both as a link with the present and a reminder of the differences of yesterday. § 132 besides being redolent of the theatre of the nineties is interesting as well for the student of poster art—the English theatre bills of the nineties seem much nearer to the world of Toulouse-Lautrec.

§ 133 (cf. p. 123)

'The City' in 1897. From a photograph of 1897 by Mr. Tom Bright. Reproduced by courtesy of Mr. H. A. Mills through Aerofilms, Ltd.

Taken at the time of Queen Victoria's Diamond Jubilee (preparation for the decorations and stands can be seen in the background) this photograph gives a view of Queen Victoria

Street, its traffic, its passers-by. Note how drab dress has become, how workaday the world appears in comparison with Shotter Boys' or Shepherd's London. (Cf. § 78, 79 and 80.)

§ 134 (cf. text p. 123)

A London Park. From a photograph by Mr. Tom Bright. Reproduced by courtesy of Mr. H. A. Mills through Aerofilms, Ltd.

This London Park has not been identified but the photograph is chosen to show the dress of the period, the sober middle class promenade as distinct from the du Maurier sketches of fashionable London society.

§ 135 (cf. text p. 125)

'The end of the Queen's last Journey.' From the *Illustrated London News* of 9 February 1901.

The death of Queen Victoria in 1901 marked the closing of an epoch, as well as the end of a remarkable and dominant personality, and as such it is chosen to conclude this volume. It shows the funeral procession leaving Windsor Castle for the Royal Mausoleum at Frogmore.

It may be remarked that except for her incidental appearance in the background of § 55 and in § 77 at the opening of the Great Exhibition, Queen Victoria is nowhere directly pictured in this volume. This is partly because I have preferred to let her speak through the atmosphere and events of her reign rather than through her portraits, to let the Prince Consort (who had such a great influence on her life), her own beloved Balmoral, the Great Exhibition, Society and the London scene from the thirties to the nineties set forth what the Victorian age meant, rather than to expect the well-known portraits of her as girl, as matron or as widow to convey any sense of the greatness and the limitations of her own personality or of her world.

Text illustration, p. 46.

'Gallop among the Bishops' (1851). By Leech from *Later Pencillings from Punch* (1865). From a copy in the Cambridge University Library.

During the fifties *Punch* concerned itself very much with ecclesiastical reform—the discrepancy between rich livings and indigent curacies, Puseyism and 'Popish' church furnishings, and Sunday observance. A selection of these by Leech are given here (cf. textual illustrations on pp. 52 and 53).

*Punch's* attitude towards 'Popery' brought about Doyle's resignation from the paper, and his reactions to the controversy may be deduced from the illustration (on p. 54) showing a

Christian Gentleman denouncing the Pope in Exeter Hall. (For a note on J. Leech cf. note to § 75.)

Text illustration p. 47

'Mother Church putting her own house in order' (1850). By J. Leech from *Early Pencillings from Punch* (1864). From a copy in the Cambridge University Library.

*Punch* applauded the removal of 'Popish' furnishings in order to provide payment for the poorer clergy. This is one of many anti-Romanist cartoons about this time. (For a general note on Leech cf. note to § 75.)

Text illustration p. 52

'Puritan Sunday or what we must all come to' (1850). By J. Leech from *Early Pencillings from Punch* (1864). From a copy in the Cambridge University Library.

The occasion of this cartoon was Lord Ashley's motion for the discontinuance of Post Office labour on Sunday: *Punch* foresees the Bishop being forced to black his own boots, if Sunday observance is carried to its logical conclusion. (For a general note on Leech cf. note to § 75.)

Text illustration p. 53

'Please, Mr. Bishop, which is Popery and which is Puseyism?' (1851). By J. Leech from *Early Pencillings from Punch* (1864). From a copy in the Cambridge University Library.

*Punch* was always eager to point out Romish leanings and here suggests that the High Church (or Anglo-Catholic) party in the Established Church (led by Pusey) was really indistinguishable from the Roman Church itself, to which Newman had already been converted. (For a general note on Leech cf. note to § 75.)

Text illustration p. 54

Popular outburst against 'Papal aggression.' From Richard Doyle's *Manners and Customs of ye Englyshe* (1849–50). From a copy in the Cambridge University Library.

Popular opinion was greatly roused by the Papal Bull of 1850 and the pastoral letter of Cardinal Wiseman (Archbishop Designate of Westmister), assuming the extension of papal rule over England. The reply to this was the Ecclesiastical Titles Bill of 1851, which prevented Roman Catholic bishops assuming ecclesiastical titles taken from any place in the United Kingdom. Public feeling ran high and the spirit of intolerance was strong. The Queen herself wrote:—'I much regret the unchristian and intolerant spirit exhibited by many people at the public meetings.'

Doyle himself broke with *Punch* over its attitude to 'Popery' and this woodcut pokes quiet fun at the audience gathered to hear 'A Christian Gentleman denouncynge ye Pope' in Exeter Hall. (For a general note on Doyle cf. note to § 70–74.)

Text illustration p. 62

'The Royal Academy Exhibition.' From Richard Doyle's *Manners and Customs of ye Englyshe* (1849–50). From a copy in the Cambridge University Library.

Doyle has drawn for us the Royal Academy's summer exhibition in its heyday: the pictures on the wall speak for themselves, so do the visitors—the fashionable, the connoisseur (peering through his glass), the eccentric and the aesthetic. (For a general note on Doyle cf. note to § 70–74.)

Text illustration p. 69

'A Railway Station, showynge ye Travellers Refreshynge themselves.' From Richard Doyle's *Manners and Customs of ye Englyshe* (1849–50). From a copy in the Cambridge University Library.

Before the days of railway dining-cars the train stopped at certain stations for a meal to be taken. This plate shows a halt at Reading, the whole train-load has turned out to snatch a meal and can be seen devouring pies and legs of chicken at the station buffet. On the platform the Guard rings his bell to warn passengers that the train is about to start. An agitated rush of travellers takes place in the background. We can almost hear the pandemonium and share the indigestion of the travellers. (For a general note on Doyle cf. note to § 70–74.)

Text illustration p. 71

Rowland Hill's 'Triumphal entry into St. Martin-le-Grand's' (1849). By J. Leech from *Early Pencillings from Punch* (1864). From a copy in the Cambridge University Library.

Rowland Hill, schoolmaster and son of a schoolmaster, set out his postal proposals in a pamphlet in 1837, on the thesis that the smaller the postal fee charged, the greater the number of users would be and hence the larger the profits of the Post Office. A uniform fee of one penny per half ounce, whatever the distance, was to be charged. The Post Office authorities condemned the plan, the Postmaster General calling it the wildest and most extravagant scheme ever heard. However, the Chancellor of the Exchequer (Mr. Spring Rice) had the courage and acumen to make provision in his Budget and the proposals were adopted. Postal charges in force prior to this were based on distance and could not be prepaid: members of the Government and

Parliament, however, could frank their own, their families' and friends' letters, for free conveyance; a practice obviously open to criticism. (For a general note on Leech cf. note to § 75.)

Text illustration p. 73

'The Gold Rush. The Road Sweeper off to California' (1849). By J. Leech from *Early Pencillings from Punch* (1864). From a copy in the Cambridge University Library.

The full tide of emigration followed the opening up of the gold fields in California and Australia. Here a road sweeper sets off to make his golden fortune. Another kind of emigrant can be seen in § 92. (For a general note on Leech cf. note to § 75.)

Text illustration p. 76

'A Banquet showynge ye Farmers Friend impressynge on ye Agricultural interest that it is ruined.' From Richard Doyle's *Manners and Customs of ye Englyshe* (1849–50). From a copy in the Cambridge University Library. (Cf. note to § 90–92.)

Up to 1815 English farming had the benefit of the high price of corn due to the Napoleonic Wars, the Corn Laws themselves being passed in 1815 to protect the farmer against low-priced imports of corn resulting from the rapid fall in price after the war. As already described in the note to § 90–92 the repeal of the Corn Laws came in 1846, necessitated by the poverty and unrest of the labouring classes. This policy naturally displeased the farmer and landowner, Doyle in this woodcut shows well-fed diners (with a sumptuous spread in front of them) giving ready ear to the prophecy of their impending ruin. (For a general note on Doyle cf. note to § 70–74.)

Text illustration p. 87

'The Navvy' (1855). By J. Leech from *Later Pencillings from Punch* (1865). From a copy in the Cambridge University Library.

'Terrible conditions in the Army in the Crimea being greatly increased for want of roads a corps of navvies was sent out.' (Cf. § 96 and 97 for illustrations of conditions in the Crimea.) (For a general note on Leech cf. note to § 75.)

Text illustration pp. 98, 99

'Reformed' taste in interior decoration (1868). Designs by Charles L. Eastlake from his *Hints on Household Taste* (1868). From a copy in the Department of Printed Books, British Museum.

In this book on 'reformed' taste, the author lays down that 'Every article of furniture should at the first glance, proclaim its real purpose.' In discussing bedroom furniture he says that modern bedrooms are as a rule too fussy in their fitting up; iron bedsteads should not be painted but a canopy and head curtains may be made to contribute 'not a little to the picturesqueness of a modern bedroom.' Coverlets should be washable, he thinks the kind of counterpanes seen in servants' bedrooms much the best, and decries petticoats for dressing tables, and bulged or shaped fronts for furniture.

Of the mantelpiece shelves he says 'A little museum may thus be formed and remain a source of lasting pleasure to its possessors.' Of the sideboard 'The general arrangement of an ordinary English sideboard is reasonable enough' he comments. He proclaims against varnish for wood carving and particularly against machine-made ornament with an artificial lustre.

These designs and comments are of particular interest when viewed against the examples of furniture and taste in the Great Exhibition's Catalogue of 1851. Though it should always be remembered that by its very nature the Great Exhibition attracted the tour de force, the ingeniously contrived, the outré.

# INDEX

ABERCROMBY, Sir Ralph, 36
Ackermann's prints, 40
Adult education movement, 16-17
Aeroplane, the, 124
Agnosticism, 29, 44, 104, 109
Agricultural labourer, 6-7, 11, 77, 80, 93, 94; housing, 8, 79-80; unions, 80; wages, 8-9, 13; standard of life, 8-9, 79, 80; in Northern counties, 7, 9, 26; and the Franchise, 94, 116
Agriculture: open-field cultivation, 76; enclosure, 76; improvement in, 75-7; great estate system, 74, 115; the Corn Laws, 3; Repeal, and after, 65, 73, 75, 79; peak of prosperity for, 80; collapse, 80, 91-5, 115
Albert Edward, Prince of Wales, 109
Albert, Prince Consort, 61, 70-1
Allotment movement, 79
Althorp, Lord, 39n., Factory Act, 82
America, South: frozen meat from, 93
America, United States of, 2, 86, 96, 122, 123
American Civil War, 96, 123
American Colonies, the, 122
American War of 1812-15, 2-3
American foodstuffs imports, 73, 91, 115, 116
Andersen, Hans, 84
Anglican School maintenance, 50
Anglo-Catholicism, 53 and n., 105; ritualistic side, 53n.
Annual Register, 29
Anti-Jacobinism, 1, 6, 17, 18, 20, 30-2, 42, 45
Anti-Slavery movement, 30-2, 42, 81; Yorkshire championship of, 31-2
Apprenticeship, 18
Arabian Nights, 84
Arch, Joseph, 80
Archaeology, 107
Architecture: Victorian era, 61-2; mass production, 62;
Aristocracy: Victorian, 90, 102, 108
Armstrong's Elswick, 99
Army: period of popularity, 35-6, 38; Wellington's, 35-7; causes of enlistment, 35; discipline and conditions

in, 35, 37; officers, 35-7; an aristocratic institution, 37, 38, 89; N.C.O.'s, the, 36; barrack accommodation, 37; and the militia, 37; standing army, 37; Reform, 89; Victorian views on, 37, 89, 123
Arnold, Matthew, 54, 58, 75, 96, 104; and 'Philistines,' 54, 58; 'barbarians,' 58
Arnold, Dr. Thomas, 48, 57-8
Arnott, Dr., 66
Art: Victorian era, 109; and photography, 111. See also Painters, Painting
Art for Art's sake, 109
Atheism, 28, 29, 109
Austen, Jane, 24; novels of, 24-5, 35
Australia, 12, 100; gold discoveries in, 72; British emigration to, 12, 86, 87, 122; frozen meat from, 93
Ayr, 98

BALFOUR's Education Bill (1902), 107n., 120, 121
Balkans, the, 88
Baptists, 29
Baring, the Banker, 3
Barrie, Sir J. M., 84
Barrow, 72n., 98
Beards, wearing of, 88
Bedfords, Earls and Dukes of, 79
Bentham, Jeremy, 31, 42
Benthamism, 46, 78, 83
Berkhamsted Common, 76
Besant, Mrs. Annie, 103
Bewick, Thomas, 10, 60
Bible, the, 18, 105; reading of, and religion, 105; inspiration of, 105-6; impact of Darwinism, 59, 106
Bicycles, 100
Birkbeck, Dr., 16
Birmingham, 118
Birth control, 103
Bishops, the, and the Reform Bill, 48
Blackpool, 100
Blomfield, Bishop, 49
Board of Education, 55, 121
Board Schools, 120